Raising
STRONG
Kids

How to Transform Difficult and Strong-Willed Children Into
Confident, Resilient Kids.

Written by

ERIC LEBOUTHILLIER

AcraPublishing | 2025 1st Edition

Preface

Parenting is one of the most rewarding yet challenging journeys we will ever take. Every child comes into the world with a unique personality, and while some are easygoing, others are strong-willed, spirited, or even difficult to understand. Parents of these children often feel exhausted, discouraged, or uncertain about how to guide them. But behind every struggle lies a powerful opportunity: the chance to raise a child who is not only resilient, but strong, confident, and ready to thrive in an unpredictable world.

This book was written with one clear belief: difficult children are not broken — they are brimming with potential. With the right guidance, their intensity can transform into determination, their defiance into leadership, and their struggles into strength. My goal is to provide you with the tools, strategies, and encouragement to help your child grow into the best version of themselves — and to remind you that you, too, are capable of rising stronger as a parent.

Who this book is for

This book is for parents, guardians, and caregivers who:

- Are raising strong-willed, spirited, or "difficult" children and want practical solutions that actually work.
- Feel overwhelmed, drained, or unsure how to set healthy boundaries while still showing love and respect.
- Want to raise children who are not only obedient, but also **confident, resilient, and emotionally intelligent**.
- Believe that their child's challenges can be turned into strengths with the right parenting approach.
- Are committed to growing alongside their child and creating a home filled with connection, respect, and trust.

What to expect from this book

Inside this book, you will discover:

- **The truth about difficult children** — why they behave the way they do, and how to see their challenges as hidden strengths.
- **Practical strategies for discipline** that focus on teaching, not punishing — helping your child learn responsibility and self-control.
- **Communication techniques** that transform yelling and conflict into cooperation and understanding.
- **Resilience-building tools** that prepare your child to handle life's setbacks with confidence and courage.
- **Step-by-step guidance for parents** — how to stay calm, set clear boundaries, and lead with both love and firmness.
- **Real-world examples and scenarios** to help you apply the lessons to your daily family life.

By the end of this book, you'll have a new perspective on parenting — one that empowers you to guide your child from difficult behaviors toward strength, confidence, and resilience.

Any trademarks, service marks, product names, or named features referenced in this book are the property of their respective owners. The author and publisher make no claim of ownership and do not endorse any third-party products or services by including them in this publication.

LEGAL DISCLAIMER

This publication is intended solely for informational and educational purposes. It does not constitute legal, financial, medical, or professional advice. The content is not a substitute for consultation with qualified experts or licensed professionals in the relevant fields.

Portions of this work have been created or assisted by artificial intelligence (AI) tools. While every reasonable effort has been made to review, fact-check, and edit the content for clarity and accuracy, AI-generated information may occasionally contain errors, omissions, or generalized statements. The author and publisher do not guarantee the accuracy, completeness, or reliability of the information provided.

Readers are strongly encouraged to seek independent advice tailored to their personal circumstances from qualified legal, financial, healthcare, or compliance professionals before making decisions or taking action based on this content.

References to specific products, services, companies, websites, or technologies do not imply endorsement or affiliation unless explicitly stated. All trademarks and brand names mentioned remain the property of their respective owners.

The author and publisher disclaim any liability, loss, or risk incurred directly or indirectly from the use or misuse of this publication. This includes, but is not limited to, damages of any kind — including incidental, special, or consequential — arising out of the reliance on the material presented.

Table of Contents

CHAPTER 1

Understanding the "Difficult" Child

Strong-willed vs. Difficult: The Real Difference

Parenting often feels like walking a tightrope. On one side is the desire to nurture your child's individuality, independence, and strength; on the other is the urgent need to maintain peace, structure, and order at home. Nowhere is this tension more visible than when raising a child who challenges boundaries, argues against rules, and insists on doing things their own way. Many parents describe such children as "difficult," but here lies the first trap: labeling a child as difficult can shape not only how you see them, but also how they begin to see themselves. In reality, many children who appear difficult are actually strong-willed. Understanding the difference between being difficult and being strong-willed is the first step in shifting how you approach discipline, guidance, and connection. It is also a crucial step in helping your child grow into their best self rather than being confined by negative labels.

Why the Distinction Matters

Words carry weight, especially when applied to children. A "difficult child" sounds like a burden, a problem to be solved, or a challenge to endure. A "strong-willed child," on the other hand, conveys persistence, determination, and inner strength—qualities that, when guided properly, can become the foundation of future success. The difference is not just semantic. It affects your mindset as a parent and ultimately the strategies you use in raising your child. If you see your child as difficult, you may unconsciously approach interactions from a place of resistance, frustration, or defensiveness. Every outburst feels like proof that your child is hard to manage, every disagreement reinforces the idea that they are difficult. But if you begin to see them as strong-willed, you shift from defensiveness to curiosity. You begin asking: What drives their resistance? How can their determination be channeled? What lessons can I teach them about balance, respect, and self-control? The framing alters your responses, and your responses in turn shape the child's behavior.

Traits of a Strong-willed Child

Strong-willed children are often misunderstood because their traits, while challenging in daily life, are the very qualities that later translate into leadership, creativity, and resilience. Some common characteristics include:

1. **Determination:** Once they decide on something, they do not easily back down. This can look like stubbornness, but it is also persistence.
2. **High Energy:** They seem to operate at full throttle, pouring intensity into their interests and their objections alike.
3. **Questioning Nature:** They ask "why" constantly and rarely accept "because I said so" as an answer.
4. **Independence:** They want to do things on their own, even if it takes longer or leads to mistakes.
5. **Emotional Intensity:** Their joys are exuberant, their frustrations loud, their anger fiery. They feel everything deeply.
6. **Strong Sense of Justice:** They often notice unfairness quickly and may protest loudly when they feel wronged, even if others dismiss it.

When you recognize these traits, you begin to see the child not as rebellious for the sake of defiance but as someone who possesses qualities that require careful nurturing. A determined, questioning, justice-driven child can grow into a tenacious adult who challenges the status quo, fights for fairness, and pursues goals relentlessly. But without guidance, the same traits can create friction, strained relationships, and cycles of conflict.

Traits of a Truly Difficult Child

To contrast, let's look at what might be considered genuinely difficult behavior. A difficult child is not simply strong-willed; instead, their behavior patterns consistently disrupt relationships, routines, and self-regulation without the compensating drive that strong-willed children display. Traits might include:

1. **Chronic Defiance Without Direction:** Resistance is constant, but not tied to independence or conviction—it's more about avoiding effort or responsibility.
2. **Low Frustration Tolerance:** Instead of persistence, there is quick giving up, paired with explosive reactions to obstacles.
3. **Frequent Disruptions:** Their behavior often derails not just their own activities but also family harmony or classroom dynamics.
4. **Limited Self-awareness:** They struggle to recognize the impact of their behavior on others and may lack empathy in the moment.
5. **Avoidance Rather Than Engagement:** Instead of channeling energy into projects or ideas, they may disengage, withdraw, or resist any form of direction.

This distinction does not mean a difficult child is doomed to struggle. It means they need different strategies: more scaffolding for self-regulation, more intentional teaching of empathy and cause-and-effect, and perhaps more support from professionals when underlying conditions such as ADHD, learning challenges, or trauma are involved.

Real-World Example: Two Children, Two Outcomes

Consider the story of Maya and Leo. Both were labeled "difficult" by their preschool teachers. Maya constantly challenged her teacher's rules, refused to sit still during circle time, and insisted on doing crafts her own way. Leo, on the other hand, often refused to participate at all. He would shut down when asked to follow instructions, throw tantrums when frustrated, and sometimes lash out at classmates.

At first glance, both seemed equally hard to manage. But when you look closer, their behaviors came from different roots. Maya's resistance was driven by a strong sense of independence and curiosity—she wanted to understand why the rules existed and preferred to explore on her own terms. With guidance, her questioning nature could become a strength in problem-solving.

Leo's behaviors, however, stemmed from low frustration tolerance and avoidance of challenging tasks. His "no" was less about independence and more about fear of failure.

The strategies needed for each child differed. Maya needed a teacher who could provide choices within boundaries and explain the reasoning behind rules, channeling her determination into leadership roles in the classroom. Leo needed structured support, encouragement for small successes, and consistent scaffolding to build confidence in tackling tasks. Labeling both as "difficult" masked their unique needs and strengths.

The Role of Parental Perception

Parents are the mirrors in which children first see themselves. If a child is constantly referred to as stubborn, troublemaking, or difficult, they may internalize those labels. Over time, these labels can become self-fulfilling prophecies. A child who believes they are "the difficult one" may give up on trying to behave differently, reasoning that they will be seen that way no matter what.

On the other hand, reframing stubbornness as persistence or defiance as independence can alter the child's own self-image. Imagine the difference between telling your child, "You're so difficult" versus, "You have such a strong sense of what you want—it's powerful. Let's figure out how to use that strength respectfully." The latter affirms their qualities while guiding their expression.

Psychological Insights: Temperament and Growth

Research in child psychology highlights that temperament—the biologically based differences in how children react to the world— plays a major role in whether a child appears strong-willed or difficult. Some children are naturally more intense, more sensitive, or more reactive. These traits are not flaws; they are part of their neurological wiring. What matters most is how parents and caregivers respond.

The concept of **"goodness of fit"** is crucial here. A child's temperament interacts with their environment, and the match between the two determines outcomes. A strong-willed child paired with an inflexible, authoritarian parent may escalate into constant battles. The same child paired with a firm but empathetic parent may flourish, learning to channel intensity into achievement. Similarly, a child with low frustration tolerance paired with patient, supportive caregivers can gradually build resilience, whereas the same child in a harsh, punitive environment may spiral into greater avoidance and acting out.

Actionable Strategies for Parents

1. **Reframe Labels:** When tempted to say "my child is difficult," pause and describe the specific behavior instead. Is your child persistent, energetic, curious, or sensitive? Precision in language leads to precision in parenting.
2. **Channel Energy:** Give strong-willed children opportunities to make choices, lead small projects, or take responsibility. Their need for autonomy can be satisfied constructively.
3. **Set Clear Boundaries:** Strong-willed does not mean rule-free. In fact, children thrive when limits are consistent and predictable. The key is enforcing rules calmly and explaining why they exist.
4. **Model Self-Regulation:** Show your child how to handle frustration by narrating your own strategies: "I feel frustrated, so I'm taking a breath before I respond."
5. **Celebrate Strengths:** Highlight how their persistence, creativity, or sense of justice can be used positively. Reinforce that their traits are not problems, but tools they are learning to use wisely.
6. **Adjust Expectations:** For children whose behavior crosses into truly difficult patterns, focus on progress rather than perfection. Small steps in regulation and cooperation are victories.

When to Seek Extra Support

Sometimes what appears to be strong-willed behavior may overlap with behavioral or developmental challenges. If your child's defiance or emotional outbursts consistently interfere with school, friendships, or family functioning, it may be wise to consult with a pediatrician, child psychologist, or counselor. Support is not about labeling your child negatively, but about equipping both you and your child with tools to manage challenges effectively.

Strong-willed Children in History

History is full of individuals who were once described as stubborn or difficult in childhood but grew into influential leaders and innovators. Thomas Edison's teachers considered him unruly and hard to manage, yet his persistence led to countless inventions. Oprah Winfrey recalls being labeled rebellious in her youth, but that same determination helped her break barriers in media. What these stories reveal is that the traits that frustrate parents in childhood often become the very qualities that allow individuals to lead, innovate, and persevere against obstacles. The challenge for parents is to recognize potential where others see problems.

Final Takeaway

The difference between a strong-willed child and a difficult child is not about how much they challenge you, but about the underlying qualities driving their behavior. Strong-willed children resist because they feel deeply, desire independence, and hold fast to their convictions. Difficult behaviors, by contrast, often signal struggles with regulation, frustration tolerance, or deeper issues that require support. Recognizing this difference changes everything. It allows you to shift from viewing your child as a problem to be managed to seeing them as a person with strengths to be guided. When you reframe their intensity as potential, you begin parenting not from fear or frustration, but from hope and strategy. You teach your child that their strongest qualities, though challenging now, are the seeds of their future resilience, leadership, and individuality. In doing so, you move from surviving parenting to thriving within it—and you give your child the gift of seeing themselves not as difficult, but as strong.

Why Children Resist Authority and Limits

Every parent has experienced the frustration of telling a child what to do and being met with outright refusal, endless negotiation, or a dramatic meltdown. From the toddler who screams when told to put on shoes to the teenager who rolls their eyes and ignores curfew, resistance to authority is a near-universal experience in parenting. But while it often feels like defiance for the sake of defiance, resistance is rarely random. Children push back against authority and limits because it fulfills psychological needs, developmental drives, or emotional responses that are deeply rooted in how human beings grow. Understanding why resistance happens is the first step in addressing it effectively—not with endless power struggles, but with strategies that strengthen trust, cooperation, and growth.

The Developmental Drive for Autonomy

One of the most powerful reasons children resist authority is that autonomy—the need to act independently and exert control over one's environment—is a fundamental part of human development. Psychologists Edward Deci and Richard Ryan, creators of **Self-Determination Theory**, identified autonomy as one of three basic psychological needs alongside competence and relatedness. In other words, children are wired to push for independence because it is essential for their growth.

This is why toddlers insist on doing things "by myself," even when it means spilling juice all over the table. It is why preschoolers argue about bedtime, and why teenagers push against curfews. In each case, the child is not only resisting rules; they are practicing independence. Resistance is a rehearsal for adulthood, a way of learning how to make decisions, take responsibility, and test the boundaries of their own competence.

For parents, this developmental drive can feel like defiance. But reframing it as practice for independence helps shift perspective. When a child argues about wearing a coat, they are not simply trying to annoy you; they are experimenting with control over their body and choices. The question is not whether they will resist—it is how parents can guide that resistance in ways that teach responsibility without crushing the child's need for autonomy.

The Psychology of Power Struggles

Resistance is not just about autonomy; it is also about power. Children quickly learn that refusing to comply is one of the few ways they can exert influence in a world largely controlled by adults. This is particularly true in homes where rules are strict and negotiation is rare. In such settings, resistance can become a child's way of saying, "I matter. I have a voice."

Consider six-year-old Aria, whose parents constantly direct her day: when to wake up, what to eat, what to wear, what activities to join, and when to go to bed. While structure is important, the lack of choice leaves Aria with little sense of control. So she digs in her heels about small things—refusing to eat dinner, protesting at bath time, or throwing tantrums when told to clean up toys. The more her parents insist, the louder she resists. What looks like disobedience is actually a child's attempt to carve out a sense of power in a world that often feels overwhelming.

Psychologists call this phenomenon **reactance**—the instinctive resistance people feel when they perceive their freedom is being restricted. Even adults experience this. If you are told you "must" do something, you are more likely to feel resistant, even if you were already inclined to do it. Children, who are still learning emotional regulation, experience reactance even more strongly. This means that heavy-handed commands or rigid rules often backfire, escalating resistance rather than reducing it.

Emotional Triggers Behind Resistance

Not all resistance stems from developmental drives or power struggles. Sometimes, children resist because of emotional triggers. When kids feel overwhelmed, anxious, or unheard, their capacity to follow directions shrinks.

For example, a child who resists homework may not be lazy or oppositional; they may be struggling with feelings of inadequacy or fear of failure. A child who refuses to leave the playground may not simply be disobedient; they may be expressing sadness about ending something they enjoy or anxiety about transitioning to a less enjoyable activity. Resistance, in these cases, is the outward expression of inner emotions that the child may not yet have the words to articulate.

Parents who respond only to the surface behavior miss the underlying message. Instead of asking, "Why won't my child listen?" a more productive question is, "What feelings are fueling this resistance?" This shift moves the focus from control to connection, opening space for empathy and problem-solving.

Cultural Influences on Authority

How children respond to authority is also shaped by cultural context. In some cultures, obedience is emphasized as a core value, and children are socialized early to defer to adults without question. In others, independence and self-expression are prioritized, making questioning authority not only tolerated but encouraged.

Neither approach is inherently right or wrong, but cultural expectations play a powerful role in how resistance is interpreted. A child who asks "why" constantly may be seen as disrespectful in one context and as curious in another. Parents who are aware of these cultural lenses can better evaluate whether their child's resistance is truly problematic or simply a reflection of different values about authority and autonomy.

The Role of Temperament

Every child comes into the world with a unique temperament—a biologically based way of responding to the environment. Some children are naturally more adaptable and easygoing, while others are intense, sensitive, or slow to warm up. A child's temperament heavily influences how they respond to authority.

For example, a highly adaptable child might accept new rules or changes in routine without much pushback, while a strong-willed child with a high activity level and strong emotional intensity might resist even small limits. Neither temperament is better or worse, but recognizing the role of temperament helps parents tailor strategies. Expecting a highly spirited child to respond with the same compliance as an easygoing sibling is a recipe for frustration. Instead, parents must adapt their expectations and techniques to fit the child they have, not the child they imagined.

Resistance as Communication

One of the most important insights for parents is this: resistance is communication. When a child refuses to do something, argues, or melts down, they are telling you something—about their needs, emotions, or perceptions of fairness.

Consider nine-year-old Jalen, who constantly resists bedtime. His parents assumed he was being oppositional, but when they finally sat down to talk with him, they discovered he was anxious about being alone in the dark. His resistance was not about disobedience but about fear. Once his parents acknowledged his feelings and provided a nightlight and calming routine, the resistance faded.

When parents learn to interpret resistance as a form of communication rather than defiance, they open the door to deeper understanding and problem-solving.

Strategies for Reducing Resistance

1. **Offer Choices Within Limits:** Instead of issuing commands, provide structured options. "Do you want to brush your teeth before or after putting on pajamas?" Giving children a sense of control reduces reactance while still ensuring the goal is met.
2. **Explain the Why:** Children are more likely to cooperate when they understand the reasoning behind rules. Explaining safety, fairness, or long-term consequences builds trust and reduces blind defiance.
3. **Validate Feelings:** Even if the rule stands, acknowledging the child's feelings about it helps reduce resistance. "I know you're upset about leaving the park—it's hard to stop having fun."
4. **Pick Battles Wisely:** Not every rule is worth a power struggle. Focus on non-negotiables like safety and respect, and allow flexibility on smaller matters.
5. **Model Respect for Authority:** Children learn from what they see. If they watch you openly disrespecting authority figures, they are more likely to imitate that behavior. Modeling thoughtful respect teaches them how to balance independence with cooperation.
6. **Build Routines:** Predictable structures reduce resistance by making expectations clear. A child who knows bedtime always follows the same steps is less likely to protest than one who is surprised by shifting rules.

When Resistance Signals Deeper Issues

Most resistance is a normal part of development, but sometimes persistent and extreme defiance may signal underlying issues such as Oppositional Defiant Disorder (ODD), ADHD, anxiety, or learning challenges. If your child's resistance is constant, intense, and disruptive across multiple settings (home, school, social life), seeking professional guidance can provide clarity and support.

Reframing Resistance as Growth

Ultimately, resistance to authority and limits is not a flaw—it is a sign of growth. Children who push back are practicing skills they will need as adults: asserting themselves, questioning rules, and navigating conflicts. The goal is not to eliminate resistance, but to guide it. Parents who understand the "why" behind resistance are better equipped to respond with strategies that teach respect, cooperation, and self-regulation, without crushing the child's spirit.

Final Takeaway

Children resist authority and limits because they are wired to grow toward independence, because they crave a sense of control, because emotions overwhelm them, and because temperament shapes how they respond to the world. Resistance is not a sign that something is broken in your child; it is a sign that they are learning, testing, and developing. The task of parenting is not to stamp out resistance but to transform it—shaping it into responsibility, empathy, and wisdom. When you see resistance not as rebellion but as rehearsal for adulthood, you begin to guide your child not with fear, but with patience and purpose.

Common Triggers of Challenging Behavior

Every parent has wondered at some point, "Why did my child just do that?" A calm morning can unravel into chaos over the wrong color cup. A simple request to put on shoes can trigger tears, yelling, or outright refusal. These moments often feel random, but in reality, challenging behaviors usually have predictable triggers. When parents identify what sparks resistance, tantrums, or defiance, they shift from reacting in frustration to responding with understanding. Recognizing common triggers not only helps prevent conflict but also teaches children valuable lessons in self-awareness and regulation.

The Hidden Role of Unmet Needs

At the core of many behavioral challenges are unmet basic needs. Just as adults become irritable when tired, hungry, or stressed, children—whose brains are still developing the capacity for self-regulation—react even more strongly. What looks like defiance may simply be exhaustion, what looks like aggression may stem from hunger, and what looks like laziness may be overwhelm.

Hunger and Blood Sugar Crashes: Children's smaller bodies and faster metabolisms mean that their blood sugar levels dip more quickly than adults'. Low blood sugar can trigger irritability, poor focus, and impulsive behavior. Many parents notice that meltdowns often happen right before meals or snacks. Instead of seeing these moments as disobedience, recognizing them as "hanger" can prompt a simple solution: a healthy snack.

Sleep Deprivation: Sleep is foundational for emotional regulation. When children are overtired, their brains struggle to manage frustration, leading to more tantrums, defiance, or silliness at inappropriate times. For example, a preschooler who refuses to leave the playground at 5 p.m. may not be testing authority as much as battling sheer exhaustion.

Overstimulation: In today's busy world, children are bombarded with noise, lights, screens, and constant activity. For sensitive children, overstimulation can quickly lead to shutdowns or explosive behavior. That meltdown in the grocery store may be less about wanting candy and more about fluorescent lights, crowds, and choices overwhelming their senses.

When parents learn to check for unmet needs before assuming disobedience, they often discover that many conflicts can be prevented with simple adjustments: snacks packed in the car, consistent sleep routines, and downtime between busy activities.

Transitions: Moving from One Thing to Another

Few things trigger resistance faster than transitions. Whether it's leaving the playground, stopping a video game, or moving from free play to homework, children often struggle with switching gears. Why? Because transitions highlight the clash between a child's current desire and an imposed external demand.

Consider eight-year-old Sam, deeply engaged in building a Lego spaceship. When his parent announces it's time for dinner, Sam explodes in anger. From the parent's perspective, it's a simple request; from Sam's perspective, it feels like being yanked away from something meaningful without warning.

The psychology here is straightforward: children have less developed executive functioning skills, the brain processes that help with planning, shifting attention, and managing impulses. Abrupt transitions overwhelm them.

Strategies to ease transitions:

- Provide **warnings**: "Five more minutes of play, then dinner."
- Use **visual timers** or countdowns so the child sees the shift coming.
- Allow **small ownership** of the transition: "Do you want to pause your game now or after you finish this level?"

Transitions will always be part of life, but with preparation and empathy, they don't have to be constant battlegrounds.

The Struggle with Control

Another common trigger of challenging behavior is the universal human desire for control. Children, like adults, want to feel that their opinions, choices, and actions matter. When they sense their control is being stripped away, resistance often follows.

Imagine four-year-old Lily at the clothing store. Her mother insists she wear the outfit she picked out. Lily screams and refuses to cooperate. What looks like rebellion is really a battle for control. By offering two acceptable options—"Do you want the red shirt or the blue one?"—the parent could give Lily a sense of agency while still guiding the outcome.

This dynamic explains why children often resist tasks they are fully capable of doing, like brushing teeth or putting on shoes. It is less about ability and more about control. For parents, the challenge is to balance structure with opportunities for autonomy, offering children meaningful choices within safe boundaries.

Emotional Overload and Stress

Children experience big feelings with little capacity to manage them. When sadness, anger, frustration, or anxiety becomes overwhelming, challenging behavior is often the outlet. For example:

- A child who lashes out during homework time may be expressing frustration over material they find confusing.
- A child who slams doors after school may be releasing pent-up stress from peer conflicts.
- A child who refuses to talk at family gatherings may be dealing with social anxiety.

Emotional overload is not misbehavior in the moral sense—it is a signal. Adults who respond with empathy ("I see you're upset; let's figure this out together") rather than punishment teach children to recognize and manage emotions instead of suppressing them.

Inconsistency and Unclear Rules

One of the most frustrating triggers for children is inconsistency. When rules change from day to day, or expectations are vague, children feel disoriented. This often leads to testing limits—not because they are inherently rebellious, but because they are searching for clarity.

For instance, if screen time is sometimes enforced strictly and other times ignored, children are more likely to argue every time. If bedtime is flexible depending on the parent's mood, children will push back to test the boundary. Clear, consistent rules reduce the need for constant negotiation and help children feel secure.

Seeking Attention

Attention is a powerful currency in childhood. When children feel ignored, they may resort to negative behaviors—whining, interrupting, or misbehaving—because even negative attention feels better than none. For example, a child who constantly interrupts adult conversations may not be trying to be rude but is signaling, "Notice me, too."

This does not mean parents should reward misbehavior with unlimited attention, but it does highlight the importance of proactive connection. Spending ten minutes of focused, positive time with a child each day often reduces attention-seeking outbursts dramatically.

Boredom and Lack of Stimulation

Children need opportunities for engagement and challenge. When bored, they may act out not from defiance but from a need for stimulation. This is especially true for high-energy or highly creative children, who may become disruptive if they lack outlets for their curiosity and energy.

A classic example is the child who constantly disrupts class—not because they cannot do the work, but because the work feels too easy. In such cases, misbehavior is a signal of unmet intellectual or creative needs. Providing more stimulating tasks, physical activity, or creative outlets can transform behavior.

Modeling and Environment

Children mirror what they see. If they witness constant conflict, yelling, or disrespect in their environment, they are more likely to act out in similar ways. Challenging behavior is often learned behavior, picked up from peers, siblings, or even adults in the home.

This is why modeling calm, respectful conflict resolution is so powerful. A parent who shouts, "Stop yelling!" unintentionally reinforces yelling as the default response. But a parent who manages frustration with calm words teaches a child how to regulate.

When Challenges Stem from Deeper Issues

While most triggers are situational or developmental, some challenging behaviors stem from underlying conditions such as ADHD, sensory processing differences, learning difficulties, or anxiety disorders. These children may appear defiant when in reality, their brains are struggling with regulation, focus, or overload. For example:

- A child with ADHD may resist sitting still not because they are disobedient, but because their brain craves movement.
- A child with sensory sensitivities may meltdown when clothing feels itchy or environments are loud.

In these cases, understanding the root cause is essential. Punishing behavior without addressing the underlying need is not only ineffective but also damaging. Professional guidance can help parents identify and support children with these challenges.

Practical Steps for Parents

1. **Observe Patterns:** Keep a simple journal of when challenging behaviors occur. Are they linked to hunger, transitions, or certain environments? Patterns reveal triggers.
2. **Plan Ahead:** Anticipate known triggers and prepare solutions—snacks in the car, transition warnings, calm-down tools.
3. **Empathize First, Correct Second:** Acknowledge the child's experience before redirecting behavior. "I know you're upset about leaving. Let's take a deep breath, then we'll go."
4. **Teach Coping Skills:** Instead of only reacting to outbursts, proactively teach children strategies—deep breathing, counting, using words—to manage big emotions.
5. **Strengthen Connection:** Invest in regular positive attention so children do not need to seek it through negative behavior.
6. **Be Consistent but Flexible:** Clear rules should be consistent, but also adaptable when genuine needs arise. For example, bedtime might be firm, but a child who is deeply engrossed in a rare book may be allowed a few extra minutes.

Final Takeaway

Challenging behaviors are rarely random. They emerge from unmet needs, difficult transitions, struggles for control, emotional overload, or unclear boundaries. When parents view these moments as signals rather than personal attacks, they move from firefighting to prevention, from frustration to understanding. Identifying triggers not only reduces conflict but also teaches children the vital skill of recognizing and managing their own needs. In this way, every meltdown, refusal, or outburst becomes not just a challenge but an opportunity for growth—for both child and parent.

The Psychology of Emotional Outbursts

Few experiences test a parent's patience like an emotional outburst. A calm afternoon can turn into chaos within seconds: a child screaming over the wrong snack, a teenager slamming doors after a simple request, or a preschooler collapsing on the floor in tears because their toy won't work. To parents, these explosions often feel irrational, excessive, and exhausting. But beneath the shouting, crying, and stomping lies something important: outbursts are not just bad behavior, they are signals of what a child's brain and emotions are struggling to process. By understanding the psychology behind emotional outbursts, parents can move from frustration to empathy and guide their children toward healthier ways of managing strong feelings.

Outbursts Are About Regulation, Not Just Behavior

When adults see a child yelling or throwing things, the natural response is to focus on the behavior. But psychology tells us that behavior is the visible tip of an iceberg; below the surface are emotions, needs, and brain processes driving the outburst. Children, especially younger ones, lack fully developed self-regulation skills. The prefrontal cortex—the part of the brain responsible for impulse control, planning, and rational decision-making—continues developing into the mid-twenties. In contrast, the amygdala—the brain's emotional alarm system—is fully active from early childhood.

This means children feel emotions strongly but lack the neurological brakes to manage them. An outburst is not a calculated act of rebellion; it is often the overflow of emotions too big for a child's current coping abilities. Parents who see outbursts only as defiance miss the deeper truth: children are not misbehaving so much as they are overwhelmed.

The Fight-or-Flight Response in Children

Outbursts are also linked to the body's stress response. When children perceive a threat—whether it is a real danger or simply the frustration of being told "no"—their nervous system activates the **fight-or-flight** response. Heart rate increases, stress hormones flood the body, and rational thought is temporarily hijacked. For adults, this can feel like road rage when someone cuts us off in traffic. For children, it might look like hitting a sibling, throwing a toy, or screaming uncontrollably.

Importantly, the child's brain in this state is not available for reasoning. Parents who try to lecture or punish mid-outburst often find it ineffective because the child is not capable of absorbing logic until the stress response has calmed. Understanding this biological process allows parents to shift from "How do I stop this right now?" to "How can I help my child regulate first, and then teach afterward?"

Triggers That Spark Outbursts

Outbursts rarely come from nowhere. Common triggers include:

1. **Frustration:** When tasks feel too hard or outcomes don't match expectations, children may erupt. A toddler unable to fit a puzzle piece, or a teen struggling with math homework, may explode in anger.
2. **Blocked Desires:** Being denied something they want—a toy, screen time, or freedom—can trigger intense disappointment, especially when children lack tools to handle "no."
3. **Transitions:** Shifting from one activity to another, especially when unprepared, often sparks meltdowns.
4. **Overstimulation:** Loud environments, crowded spaces, or too many demands at once overwhelm a child's nervous system.
5. **Accumulated Stress:** Just like adults, children carry stress from school, peers, or family life. A small trigger at home may unleash emotions bottled up all day.

By identifying triggers, parents can often prevent outbursts before they escalate.

Outbursts by Age: What's Normal?

Understanding what is developmentally typical helps parents respond with perspective.

Toddlers and Preschoolers: Emotional outbursts are frequent at this age because language and self-regulation are still developing. Tantrums over snacks, toys, or routines are common and usually signal unmet needs or frustration.

Elementary-Age Children: Outbursts may become less frequent but can still be intense, especially around school pressures, peer conflicts, or transitions. These children are beginning to grasp social rules but may lack emotional vocabulary.

Adolescents: Teens experience surges in emotional intensity due to hormonal changes and ongoing brain development. Outbursts may look different—door slamming, sarcasm, defiance—but the root is similar: emotions feel overwhelming, and regulation skills are still maturing.

Knowing what is age-appropriate prevents parents from overreacting to normal developmental struggles while still guiding children toward better coping strategies.

Emotional Outbursts as Communication

Outbursts often mask deeper feelings children cannot express in words. A tantrum over not getting a cookie may really be sadness about a tough day at preschool. A teen's angry explosion after being told to clean their room may actually reflect embarrassment about struggling in school. When children lack emotional vocabulary, their bodies and behaviors speak for them.

Parents who ask, "What might my child be trying to tell me through this outburst?" uncover needs that might otherwise go unnoticed. This perspective transforms conflict into connection. Instead of punishing the surface behavior, parents can address the underlying emotion, teaching children healthier ways to communicate.

The Role of Temperament

Not all children respond to frustration the same way. Temperament plays a major role in how prone a child is to outbursts. Children with more intense or sensitive temperaments often feel emotions more strongly and therefore have more dramatic expressions.

For example, one child may shrug off being told they cannot have candy, while another may erupt in tears and screams. Both responses are normal for that child's temperament, but the strategies needed to help will differ. Recognizing temperament prevents parents from unfair comparisons ("Why can't you be calm like your sister?") and instead allows for tailored support.

The Parent-Child Feedback Loop

Emotional outbursts often escalate because of how adults respond. When a child screams, a parent's stress rises, triggering their own fight-or-flight response. Yelling back or imposing harsh punishment in the heat of the moment creates a feedback loop where both parent and child are dysregulated.

Breaking this cycle requires adults to model calm. Neuroscience shows that children's nervous systems are influenced by co-regulation—the process of calming through another person's presence. When parents stay steady, even if firm, they help the child's nervous system return to balance. A calm adult is not just enforcing rules; they are teaching emotional regulation by example.

Why Punishment Alone Doesn't Work

Many parents instinctively punish outbursts—sending the child to their room, removing privileges, or scolding harshly. While consequences have their place, punishment alone rarely reduces emotional explosions. That's because punishment addresses the behavior without teaching the child the skills they need to handle big emotions differently next time.

It is like punishing someone for not knowing how to swim rather than teaching them swimming skills. Children need guidance in recognizing emotions, calming strategies, and problem-solving—not just penalties after the fact. Without skill-building, the cycle of outbursts simply repeats.

Building Skills to Prevent Outbursts

The most effective approach to emotional outbursts is proactive teaching. Skills can include:

1. **Emotional Vocabulary:** Helping children label feelings—angry, frustrated, disappointed—gives them words instead of explosions.
2. **Calming Strategies:** Breathing exercises, squeezing a stress ball, or taking a break provide tools for regulation.
3. **Problem-Solving:** Teaching children to ask, "What else can I do?" when frustrated builds resilience.
4. **Role Modeling:** Parents who narrate their own coping strategies ("I'm frustrated, so I'm going to take a deep breath") show children how to handle strong emotions.
5. **Consistent Routines:** Predictable structures reduce the anxiety that fuels outbursts.

A Real-World Illustration

Consider ten-year-old Malik, who frequently explodes during homework time. His parents initially assumed he was lazy or oppositional. But closer observation revealed that Malik's outbursts were triggered by feelings of shame when he didn't understand assignments. His yelling and crying were expressions of "I feel stupid" in a language he didn't yet have.

Instead of punishing the behavior, his parents worked with his teacher to provide clearer instructions and praised small successes. They also taught Malik calming strategies when frustration rose. Over time, his outbursts decreased not because he feared punishment, but because he felt more capable of handling challenges.

When Outbursts Signal Deeper Concerns

While occasional outbursts are normal, persistent, intense, or destructive explosions may indicate underlying issues such as anxiety disorders, ADHD, trauma, or mood regulation difficulties. In these cases, professional support can provide assessment and strategies. Parents should not see this as failure but as advocacy—ensuring their child has the tools and support they need to thrive.

Shifting Perspective: From Chaos to Growth

When parents view emotional outbursts only as misbehavior, the response tends to be reactive—punishment, yelling, or frustration. But when outbursts are seen as signals of developmental needs, emotional overload, or communication attempts, the response shifts to empathy and guidance. This reframing doesn't excuse destructive behavior, but it allows parents to address both the surface actions and the deeper causes.

Final Takeaway

Emotional outbursts are not signs that children are "bad" or hopelessly defiant. They are evidence that children are still learning the complex skills of self-regulation, communication, and emotional management. Outbursts reflect the imbalance between powerful feelings and limited coping tools. Parents who understand the psychology behind these explosions can respond not with shame or punishment, but with calm, empathy, and teaching. In doing so, they help children build resilience, emotional intelligence, and self-control—the very qualities that will carry them into adulthood with strength.

Recognizing Hidden Strengths in Difficult Kids

When parents describe their child as "difficult," the word usually comes with exhaustion, frustration, or even guilt. They imagine the countless tantrums, endless negotiations, and resistance to rules that seem to define daily life. But what if those very traits that feel overwhelming now are the seeds of powerful strengths later? What if the child who argues endlessly is developing strong critical thinking, or the one who refuses to back down is building resilience that will serve them for life? Recognizing the hidden strengths in children who are labeled as difficult transforms how parents respond. Instead of seeing a problem to fix, you begin to see potential to shape.

Why Strengths Are Easy to Miss

Parenting is a demanding job, and difficult behavior commands attention. The child who throws tantrums in the grocery store, argues at bedtime, or refuses to follow directions becomes the center of focus. Strengths, in contrast, are quieter and often overshadowed by disruptive moments. Parents may overlook persistence, creativity, or boldness because those qualities emerge in inconvenient or challenging ways.

Another reason strengths are overlooked is bias. Society tends to value compliance, politeness, and quietness in children. A child who questions authority, challenges norms, or insists on their own path may be labeled as trouble rather than celebrated as independent. Yet history is filled with innovators and leaders who once carried those same labels in childhood.

The Link Between Difficult Traits and Hidden Strengths

Every challenging trait has a flipside. When reframed, difficult behaviors reveal underlying qualities that, if guided, become assets.

1. **Stubbornness → Persistence**
   The child who refuses to give up during an argument may grow into an adult who refuses to give up on their dreams. Persistence is the foundation of achievement, from learning an instrument to building a career.
2. **Argumentativeness → Critical Thinking**
   Children who debate every rule are practicing reasoning skills. While exhausting for parents, this capacity to question assumptions is the same skill that drives scientific discovery and social reform.
3. **High Energy → Enthusiasm and Leadership**
   The child who cannot sit still may later become the energetic leader who motivates teams or drives projects forward. Energy, when channeled, inspires others.
4. **Emotional Intensity → Passion and Empathy**
   The child who cries loudly or celebrates wildly feels deeply. This intensity can translate into passion for causes, empathy for others, and the ability to connect on a profound level.
5. **Defiance → Strong Sense of Self**
   A child who refuses to conform blindly may grow into an adult who resists peer pressure and makes independent decisions. Defiance, when balanced with respect, becomes integrity.

By reframing difficult behaviors in this way, parents can begin to guide rather than suppress their child's natural wiring.

Real-World Example: The "Impossible" Child

Consider twelve-year-old Elena. Teachers described her as disruptive: she questioned instructions, refused to follow rules she thought were unfair, and often debated with adults. At home, she challenged bedtime routines and resisted chores. Her parents felt worn down.

But a mentor noticed something different. Elena's questions weren't mindless defiance; they were sharp, logical, and passionate. When given leadership roles in group projects, she thrived. Instead of being silenced, she was encouraged to channel her critical thinking into debate club and community service. Within a year, Elena was recognized for her leadership and advocacy. The qualities once seen as "impossible" became the foundation of her emerging strengths.

This story illustrates a crucial truth: difficult traits, when recognized as strengths, shift from being sources of conflict to pathways of growth.

The Role of Mindset: Seeing Beyond the Moment

Psychologist Carol Dweck's work on **growth mindset** applies not only to children but also to parents. A fixed mindset views a child as "difficult" and stuck in those traits, while a growth mindset sees behaviors as opportunities to develop strengths. The difference lies in perspective.

When a parent says, "My child is stubborn," the conversation often ends there. But when they reframe it as, "My child is persistent—I need to teach them when to hold on and when to let go," the door opens to growth. Mindset transforms daily frustrations into opportunities for teaching and guiding.

Hidden Strengths in Different Developmental Stages

Recognizing strengths requires understanding how traits manifest at different ages.

Toddlers: Tantrums and independence struggles may signal early determination and self-advocacy. The toddler who insists "I do it myself" is building autonomy.

Elementary-Age Children: Arguing and questioning rules often reflect growing cognitive skills. These children are beginning to understand fairness and justice.

Adolescents: Defiance and boundary-pushing signal identity formation. Teens who resist conformity are learning to define themselves apart from peers and parents.

When parents see these stages as part of growth rather than rebellion, they are better equipped to support rather than suppress their child's development.

Practical Strategies to Spot Strengths

1. **Look for Patterns in Play and Passion:** Even "difficult" children reveal strengths in activities they love. A child who argues at bedtime but spends hours building Lego sets may be demonstrating focus and creativity.
2. **Listen Beneath the Defiance:** When children resist, ask what value is driving them. A child who protests "That's not fair!" is showing a sense of justice.
3. **Ask Teachers and Mentors:** Adults outside the home often see strengths that parents, caught in daily struggles, miss.
4. **Separate the Behavior from the Trait:** Throwing a toy in anger is not a strength, but the intensity behind it may point to passion or determination. The task is to guide expression, not erase the trait.
5. **Celebrate Small Wins:** When your child channels persistence into finishing a puzzle or uses their energy to help

a sibling, highlight it. Naming strengths helps children see themselves positively.

Teaching Balance: Strengths Without Harm

Recognizing strengths does not mean excusing hurtful behavior. Persistence must be balanced with flexibility, passion with regulation, independence with respect. Parents play the role of coach, teaching children how to use their traits wisely. For example:

- Teach a stubborn child how to recognize when persistence becomes counterproductive.
- Guide an argumentative child to express ideas respectfully and listen to others.
- Help an energetic child find healthy outlets through sports or creative projects.

The goal is not to suppress traits but to shape them into strengths that serve both the child and their relationships.

Historical and Cultural Examples

History is filled with individuals once considered difficult children. Winston Churchill was described as unruly and defiant, yet his stubbornness became determination that shaped a nation during crisis. Maya Angelou, known for her boldness and strong spirit, transformed her intensity into poetry and activism that inspired generations.

Cultural context also matters. In some cultures, assertiveness in children is discouraged, while in others it is nurtured. Recognizing hidden strengths requires looking beyond cultural bias to see traits for their potential impact in adulthood.

When Strengths Need Extra Support

Sometimes, what could be a strength overwhelms the child and family. Intensity that becomes aggression, energy that turns into constant disruption, or independence that crosses into isolation may signal the need for extra support. Therapists, counselors, or mentors can help children learn to channel traits constructively. Seeking support does not diminish the child's potential; it enhances it.

Reframing for Parents: From Burden to Opportunity

Recognizing hidden strengths also transforms the parent's experience. Instead of feeling constantly at odds with their child, parents begin to see their role as guiding a powerful force. The daily battles are no longer just struggles but training grounds for future leaders, innovators, and changemakers. This shift reduces parental stress and builds patience, because frustration is replaced with purpose.

Final Takeaway

Every "difficult" child carries hidden strengths. Stubbornness is persistence, defiance is independence, intensity is passion, argumentativeness is critical thinking, and high energy is leadership in disguise. The challenge for parents is not to erase these traits but to channel them. When you recognize the strengths within the struggles, you transform conflict into growth. You give your child the gift of seeing themselves not as difficult, but as capable, resilient, and strong. And you give yourself the gift of parenting with hope, patience, and vision for the future.

CHAPTER 2

Building a Foundation of Love and Respect

The Power of Unconditional Acceptance

Every child enters the world with an invisible question: *Am I loved for who I am, or only for what I do?* The answer parents give to this question—through words, actions, and tone—shapes not only how a child sees themselves, but how they approach life, relationships, and challenges. When love and acceptance feel conditional, children learn to hide parts of themselves, to perform for approval, and to fear mistakes. When acceptance is unconditional, they feel secure, valued, and resilient. They develop the courage to take risks, the confidence to bounce back from setbacks, and the compassion to extend acceptance to others.

Unconditional acceptance is not permissiveness. It does not mean ignoring harmful behavior or eliminating boundaries. Instead, it is the steady assurance that beneath the rules, the corrections, and the struggles, the child's worth is never in question. Their behavior may need guidance, but their identity is embraced. For parents raising strong-willed or "difficult" children, this distinction is life-changing. It reframes discipline from rejection to guidance, turning conflict into connection.

Why Acceptance Is a Core Human Need

Psychological research consistently shows that the need for belonging and acceptance is as essential as food and safety. Abraham Maslow's hierarchy of needs places love and belonging directly after physiological and safety needs, highlighting how foundational acceptance is to human development. Without it, children struggle with insecurity, low self-esteem, and anxiety. With it, they develop resilience and emotional stability.

For children, acceptance functions like emotional oxygen. It allows them to explore, make mistakes, and return to the safe base of parental love. Consider a toddler learning to walk: they stumble repeatedly, but the parent's encouragement provides the confidence to keep trying. Imagine if that same toddler were scolded or shamed with each fall—the result would not be faster walking but reluctance to try again. Acceptance gives children permission to learn and grow without fear of rejection.

Conditional Love: The Hidden Danger

Many parents love their children deeply but unintentionally communicate conditional acceptance. Phrases like "I'm proud of you when you behave" or "You make me happy when you get good grades" suggest that love is tied to performance. Over time, children internalize the belief that they must earn approval.

Conditional acceptance often leads to:

1. **Perfectionism:** Children strive to meet expectations at any cost, fearing failure will make them unworthy.
2. **Hiding Mistakes:** To preserve approval, children conceal errors or struggles instead of seeking help.
3. **Fragile Self-Esteem:** Confidence becomes dependent on external validation rather than an inner sense of worth.
4. **Strained Relationships:** Conditional acceptance teaches children that relationships are transactional, making trust difficult.

The danger of conditional acceptance is subtle: it motivates in the short term but damages long-term resilience. Children may comply, but they do so out of fear rather than confidence, leaving them less prepared to face real-world challenges.

Unconditional Acceptance vs. Approval of Behavior

One common misconception is that unconditional acceptance means approving of everything a child does. In reality, unconditional acceptance separates the child's worth from their actions. Parents can reject a behavior without rejecting the child.

For example:

- Saying, "You are being so bad" communicates rejection of the child.
- Saying, "I love you, and I don't like that you hit your brother" separates identity from action.

This distinction matters because children internalize labels. Being called "bad" creates shame and identity confusion. Being told their behavior was harmful, while their worth remains intact, creates space for growth.

The Science of Secure Attachment

Attachment theory, pioneered by John Bowlby and expanded by Mary Ainsworth, shows that children who experience consistent love and acceptance develop **secure attachment**. These children trust that their caregiver is a safe base, allowing them to explore the world with confidence. Securely attached children are more resilient, emotionally balanced, and capable of healthy relationships later in life.

Conversely, when acceptance feels conditional or inconsistent, children may develop insecure attachment patterns—clinging for approval, avoiding connection, or acting out for attention. Insecure attachment is linked to anxiety, depression, and difficulties in adulthood. The foundation of secure attachment is unconditional acceptance: the assurance that no mistake, failure, or misbehavior can remove love.

Real-World Illustration: The Report Card

Consider two scenarios:

In the first, a child brings home a report card with mostly good grades but one disappointing mark. The parent's first reaction is, "Why did you get a C? You know you can do better." The child hears that love and pride are tied to performance.

In the second, the parent begins with, "I'm proud of the effort you've made, and I love you no matter what. Let's look together at how we can improve in this subject." The child hears that love is secure, and the focus shifts from shame to growth.

The difference is profound. In the first case, the child may feel pressure to hide mistakes. In the second, the child feels supported and motivated to improve.

Unconditional Acceptance in Discipline

Discipline is one of the hardest places to practice unconditional acceptance. When children misbehave, emotions run high, and rejection often slips into tone or words. But discipline rooted in unconditional acceptance focuses on teaching rather than punishment.

Practical approaches include:

1. **Calm Correction:** Address the behavior without shaming the child.
2. **Restoration Over Punishment:** Instead of isolating a child after hitting, guide them to repair the relationship with their sibling.
3. **Consistent Assurance:** Use phrases like, "I'm upset about what happened, but I always love you."
4. **After-Conflict Connection:** Reconnect after discipline to reinforce the relationship.

These strategies teach accountability while preserving the child's sense of belonging.

Hidden Strengths Unlocked by Acceptance

When children feel unconditionally accepted, their strengths shine more clearly. The strong-willed child who feels secure channels determination into goals rather than battles. The sensitive child uses empathy constructively instead of withdrawing in fear. The energetic child learns to lead rather than disrupt. Acceptance unlocks potential because it removes the burden of proving worth.

The Parent's Inner Work

Practicing unconditional acceptance is not always easy. Parents carry their own histories of conditional love, perfectionism, or rejection. These patterns can unconsciously influence how they respond to their children. Breaking the cycle requires self-awareness and healing. Parents who recognize their own wounds can choose to respond differently, giving their children the acceptance they may have longed for themselves.

Simple reflective questions include:

- "When do I feel tempted to withdraw love or approval?"
- "Am I valuing my child for who they are or only for what they achieve?"
- "How can I communicate love even in correction?"

By doing their own inner work, parents create a new legacy of acceptance for future generations.

Building Daily Practices of Acceptance

Unconditional acceptance is not a one-time declaration; it is a daily practice. Ways to communicate acceptance include:

1. **Affirmation:** Regularly tell children, "I love you just as you are."
2. **Physical Connection:** Hugs, eye contact, and gentle touch reinforce belonging.
3. **Active Listening:** Give full attention when children share, signaling that their thoughts matter.
4. **Celebrating Effort, Not Just Results:** Acknowledge persistence, creativity, or kindness, not only achievements.
5. **Quality Time:** Small, consistent moments of connection communicate value.

These practices accumulate into a strong message: *You are accepted, always.*

When Acceptance Meets Real-World Challenges

Parents often ask, "How can I practice unconditional acceptance when my child's behavior is harmful, disrespectful, or exhausting?" The key is remembering that acceptance is not approval. You can set firm boundaries, impose consequences, and express disappointment while still affirming love. In fact, unconditional acceptance makes boundaries more effective, because children understand that rules exist within a safe, loving relationship, not as a withdrawal of love.

Final Takeaway

Unconditional acceptance is one of the greatest gifts parents can give. It tells children: *You are loved not because you behave, achieve, or please me, but because you are you.* This foundation builds resilience, confidence, and emotional security. It transforms discipline from rejection into guidance, struggles into opportunities for growth, and difficult traits into strengths. Parenting with unconditional acceptance is not about being permissive—it is about anchoring your child in unwavering love so they have the courage to become their fullest selves.

How Empathy Rewires Parent–Child Relationships

Every parent knows the frustration of being ignored, argued with, or met with an emotional explosion. The instinctive response in these moments is often to demand compliance: *"Because I said so!"* Yet, while authority can enforce short-term obedience, it rarely builds long-term cooperation. What does? Empathy.

Empathy—the ability to understand and share another's feelings—changes the entire dynamic between parent and child. Neuroscience shows that empathy not only soothes emotional storms but also literally rewires the brain, shaping pathways for connection, trust, and emotional regulation. When practiced consistently, empathy transforms conflict into cooperation, resentment into respect, and distance into deep relational security.

Why Empathy Matters More Than Authority Alone

Authority enforces rules. Empathy builds relationships. Children need both, but without empathy, authority becomes rigid and brittle. A child who fears punishment may comply in the short term but resist internally, resent authority, or rebel later. A child who experiences empathy learns that their feelings are understood and valued. This does not mean they always get their way, but it does mean they feel seen.

Psychologist Daniel Siegel emphasizes that being "seen and soothed" is crucial for healthy brain development. When children feel understood, their nervous systems calm, making them more capable of learning, listening, and cooperating. In other words, empathy opens the door to influence. Without it, even the best rules fall on deaf ears.

The Neuroscience of Empathy

Modern brain research shows that empathy has measurable effects. Mirror neurons, discovered in the 1990s, activate when we observe someone else's emotions or actions, allowing us to "mirror" their experience. When parents respond empathetically, children's mirror neurons fire, teaching them how to attune to others.

Additionally, empathy calms the amygdala, the brain's fear and alarm center. When a child feels misunderstood, the amygdala stays activated, fueling fight-or-flight responses—tantrums, defiance, or withdrawal. When a parent responds with empathy, the child's brain shifts from survival mode to learning mode. Over time, repeated experiences of being soothed and understood strengthen neural pathways for regulation. In simple terms: empathy teaches the brain how to stay calm under stress.

Empathy vs. Sympathy: The Crucial Difference

Parents often confuse empathy with sympathy. Sympathy says, "I feel sorry for you." Empathy says, "I feel with you." Sympathy creates distance, while empathy creates connection. For example:

- A sympathetic response: *"You're upset about losing the game, but it's not a big deal. Don't cry."*
- An empathetic response: *"I can see how disappointed you are about losing. You really wanted to win."*

The first minimizes feelings, leaving the child alone in their experience. The second validates emotions, helping the child process them constructively.

Why Empathy Feels Hard in the Moment

Parents know empathy matters, yet practicing it in heated moments can feel impossible. Why? Because children's outbursts trigger parents' own stress responses. A screaming toddler or defiant teen activates frustration, anger, or fear in adults. Without awareness, parents react rather than respond.

Practicing empathy requires self-regulation. Parents must calm their own nervous systems before they can soothe their child's. This may mean pausing, taking deep breaths, or silently reminding yourself: *"This is not about me. My child is struggling, not attacking."* By modeling regulation, parents not only manage their own emotions but also teach children how to manage theirs.

Real-World Example: The Morning Meltdown

Consider a scenario: eight-year-old James refuses to get dressed for school. His mother, already late for work, feels her blood pressure rising. The instinctive response is to yell: *"Get dressed now or you'll lose screen time!"* James resists harder, escalating the battle.

An empathetic approach looks different. His mother kneels down, makes eye contact, and says, *"It looks like you're having a hard time getting ready today. Are you feeling tired or worried about something at school?"* James mutters that he forgot about a spelling test. Suddenly, the resistance makes sense: it was anxiety, not laziness. By naming his feelings and offering reassurance, his mother diffuses the meltdown and helps him face the day.

This example highlights how empathy moves beyond behavior to the underlying cause. Instead of battling symptoms, empathy addresses the root.

Empathy as a Discipline Tool

Many parents fear that too much empathy will lead to permissiveness. In reality, empathy strengthens discipline. Why? Because discipline means teaching, not punishing. Children learn best when they feel safe and connected. Empathy creates that foundation.

For example:

- Instead of, *"Stop hitting your sister or you'll go to your room,"* try, *"I can see you're angry with your sister. It's okay to feel angry, but it's not okay to hit. Let's find another way to tell her how you feel."*
- Instead of, *"Do your homework now!"* try, *"I know homework feels frustrating sometimes. Let's make a plan to get through it together."*

These responses do not excuse bad behavior. They acknowledge emotions while holding firm boundaries. Over time, children internalize both: *my feelings matter, and my actions have consequences.*

Teaching Empathy Through Modeling

Children learn empathy by experiencing it. When parents respond empathetically, children not only calm down but also absorb empathy as a skill. They begin to mirror it in their own relationships.

Consider a child whose parents consistently validate their feelings. When a friend at school falls and cries, that child is more likely to respond with, *"Are you okay? That must hurt,"* instead of ignoring or mocking. By contrast, children who are told to "toughen up" may learn to dismiss others' emotions as well.

Empathy, then, is not only a parenting strategy but also a gift parents pass down, shaping how children relate to siblings, peers, and eventually their own children.

The Long-Term Impact of Empathy

Empathy does more than calm meltdowns—it shapes lifelong outcomes. Research shows that children who experience empathetic parenting:

- Develop higher emotional intelligence, a predictor of success in relationships and careers.
- Show better problem-solving skills because they learn to manage emotions before tackling challenges.
- Are less likely to engage in aggressive or antisocial behavior, since empathy models constructive conflict resolution.
- Build resilience, because they feel supported in failure rather than shamed.

In contrast, children who grow up without empathy may struggle with emotional regulation, resort to aggression, or seek unhealthy ways to meet their need for connection.

When Empathy Meets Resistance

Sometimes, even empathetic responses do not produce instant cooperation. A child may continue to yell, refuse, or push boundaries. Empathy is not a magic switch; it is a practice. Over time, repeated experiences of being understood gradually reduce resistance and build trust.

Think of empathy like water smoothing rough stone. It may not reshape the surface immediately, but consistent presence transforms hardness into softness. Parents who persist in empathy teach their children that love is steady, even in conflict.

Practical Strategies to Build Empathy in Parenting

1. **Pause Before Responding:** Take a breath before reacting to give space for empathy to emerge.
2. **Get on Their Level:** Physically lowering yourself to eye level communicates respect and reduces intimidation.
3. **Name the Emotion:** Even if you guess wrong, naming feelings helps children develop emotional vocabulary.
4. **Validate Before Correcting:** Start with empathy, then move to guidance. "I see you're angry… It's not okay to hit."
5. **Practice Daily Check-Ins:** Ask, "How are you feeling today?" to normalize emotional conversations outside of crisis moments.
6. **Model Empathy With Others:** Children watch how you treat waiters, neighbors, or your spouse. Your empathy toward others teaches them as much as your empathy toward them.

A Parent's Inner Challenge

Practicing empathy also requires parents to confront their own stories. If you grew up in a home where emotions were dismissed or punished, empathy may feel unnatural. It may trigger discomfort or skepticism. But choosing empathy is a way of breaking cycles. By giving your child what you may not have received, you create a new generational pattern of connection and trust.

Final Takeaway

Empathy is not weakness, indulgence, or permissiveness. It is a powerful tool that rewires both parent and child. It calms the brain, strengthens discipline, builds trust, and teaches children to connect with others. When parents lead with empathy, they transform authority from fear-based control into respect-based influence. The result is not only better behavior in the moment but also deeper bonds and stronger character for a lifetime.

Respect as a Two-Way Street

Respect is one of the most frequently discussed values in parenting. Parents often insist, *"My child needs to respect me."* Teachers emphasize respect in classrooms, and society praises respectful children as polite, obedient, and well-mannered. Yet respect, when viewed only as one-directional—from child to parent—misses the deeper truth. Respect is not demanded; it is cultivated. It is not a one-way street; it is a reciprocal exchange. Children learn respect not by being forced into submission but by experiencing respect themselves.

When respect is mutual, power struggles decrease, communication improves, and children feel valued as human beings rather than controlled subjects. When respect is one-sided, children may comply outwardly but harbor resentment, rebellion, or indifference inwardly. To raise children who truly understand and embody respect, parents must practice it daily—not just expecting it, but modeling it.

What Respect Really Means

Respect is often confused with obedience. But true respect is broader and deeper. Obedience is doing what someone says. Respect is valuing someone's worth, opinions, and boundaries. A child can obey out of fear while secretly despising authority. Respect, by contrast, fosters cooperation rooted in trust, not fear.

For children, learning respect means learning that others have feelings, needs, and perspectives that matter. For parents, modeling respect means showing children that their voices, emotions, and individuality are valued—even when rules must be enforced.

Why Respect Cannot Be Forced

Parents can force obedience through punishment, threats, or intimidation. But forced obedience is fragile. It works only when the authority figure is present, and it often breeds rebellion when children gain independence. Respect, on the other hand, grows from consistent modeling.

Imagine a boss who yells, belittles, and demands compliance. Employees may follow instructions but do so grudgingly, avoiding initiative or loyalty. Contrast that with a boss who listens, values input, and treats employees fairly. Those employees not only cooperate but also contribute with energy and commitment. The same principle applies in families. Children who experience respect are more likely to respect their parents in return—and carry that value into all relationships.

Respect in Everyday Parenting Moments

Respect in parenting is not abstract; it shows up in small, daily interactions:

- **Listening Without Interrupting:** When a child explains why they are upset, listening fully communicates that their perspective matters.
- **Knocking Before Entering:** Simple acts like respecting privacy reinforce dignity.
- **Using a Respectful Tone:** Yelling or belittling may enforce compliance but undermines respect. Calm, firm communication models how to handle conflict respectfully.
- **Acknowledging Effort:** Respect includes recognizing children's efforts, not just outcomes.

These moments teach children more about respect than lectures ever could.

Real-World Example: The Dinner Table

Consider a family dinner where nine-year-old Ava interrupts repeatedly. A parent demanding respect might snap: *"Stop talking over people! Be quiet!"* Ava may comply, but she also feels silenced.

A respectful approach might be: *"Ava, I can see you're excited to share your idea. Let's wait until your brother finishes, then it's your turn. We all want to hear what you have to say."* This response corrects the behavior while affirming Ava's voice. She learns respect not just as a rule but as a value experienced in action.

The Psychology of Mutual Respect

Respect fosters connection because it meets children's core psychological needs. According to self-determination theory, humans thrive when they experience autonomy, competence, and relatedness. Respect satisfies all three:

- **Autonomy:** Children feel their choices and opinions matter.
- **Competence:** They feel capable when their efforts are acknowledged.

- **Relatedness:** They feel connected when their emotions are taken seriously.

By contrast, disrespect undermines these needs, leaving children feeling powerless, inadequate, or disconnected. Over time, this erodes cooperation and increases conflict.

Respect Does Not Mean Permissiveness

A common fear among parents is that showing too much respect will lead to permissiveness. But respect is not about removing boundaries; it is about enforcing them with dignity. For example:

- Disrespectful response: *"Stop whining. You're acting like a baby."*
- Respectful response: *"I hear that you're upset. It's okay to feel disappointed, but yelling isn't the way to solve it. Let's talk about what you need."*

The boundary remains firm—yelling is not acceptable—but the child's feelings are acknowledged. Respect balances authority with empathy, creating an environment where rules are internalized rather than resisted.

Respect Across Developmental Stages

Toddlers: Respect looks like offering choices ("Do you want the red cup or the blue one?") and acknowledging big emotions without shame.

Elementary-Age Children: Respect includes listening to their reasoning, even when rules remain non-negotiable. For example: "I understand you don't want to do homework now. Let's talk about when you'll get it done."

Adolescents: Respect means giving increasing independence, involving them in family decisions, and honoring their privacy.

Teens especially rebel against hypocrisy; if parents demand respect but act disrespectfully, teens will see through it instantly.

When Respect Is Absent

Children who grow up in environments lacking respect often develop one of two patterns:

1. **Compliance Without Confidence:** They obey but lack self-worth, often struggling with assertiveness in adulthood.
2. **Rebellion Without Reflection:** They reject authority entirely, often carrying resentment and mistrust into relationships.

In both cases, the absence of mutual respect undermines healthy development. By contrast, children raised with respect learn both to set boundaries for themselves and to honor the boundaries of others.

Cultural Perspectives on Respect

In some cultures, respect is equated with obedience and hierarchy, while in others it emphasizes equality and mutual understanding. Parents navigating multicultural environments may struggle with balancing these perspectives. The key is distinguishing between blind obedience and genuine respect. Children can be taught to honor elders and follow rules while still being encouraged to express their thoughts and feelings respectfully. Mutual respect bridges cultural differences by grounding authority in dignity rather than domination.

Teaching Respect Through Modeling

Children learn far more from what parents do than from what they say. If a parent yells, mocks, or belittles, children internalize those behaviors as normal. If a parent listens, apologizes when wrong, and treats others with kindness, children absorb those lessons too. Modeling respect requires humility. Saying, *"I was wrong to raise my voice. I'm sorry,"* teaches children that respect includes accountability.

Practical Strategies to Build Mutual Respect

1. **Use Respectful Language:** Avoid labels like "lazy" or "bad." Focus on specific behaviors instead.
2. **Practice Active Listening:** Repeat back what your child says to show you heard: "So you're upset because you wanted more time to play."
3. **Involve Children in Decisions:** Give them input on family rules, chores, or routines to foster ownership.
4. **Set Clear Boundaries Respectfully:** State expectations firmly but calmly, without threats or humiliation.
5. **Model Respect With Others:** Show courtesy to waiters, teachers, neighbors—children notice consistency.
6. **Repair After Conflict:** If tempers flare, reconnect afterward. A simple, *"I love you, and I want us to work better together,"* restores mutual respect.

A Parent's Inner Challenge

Mutual respect also requires parents to confront their own patterns. If you grew up in a home where respect meant blind obedience, practicing two-way respect may feel uncomfortable. It may even feel like a loss of authority. But true authority does not diminish when respect is mutual; it grows stronger. When children respect parents because they feel respected, authority becomes influence rather than control.

Final Takeaway

Respect in parenting is not about demanding obedience or silencing children. It is about building a relationship where both voices matter, where rules are enforced with dignity, and where love and authority are balanced with understanding. Respect is not a one-way street; it flows both directions. When parents model respect, they raise children who not only respect authority but also respect themselves and others. In doing so, they cultivate not just compliance, but character.

Positive Reinforcement vs. Punishment

For centuries, discipline has been equated with punishment. From time-outs to spanking, from grounding to taking away privileges, many parents have assumed that the best way to shape behavior is to make children feel bad when they misbehave. Yet modern psychology, neuroscience, and decades of research tell a different story: punishment may stop a behavior in the short term, but it rarely builds lasting change. Positive reinforcement, by contrast, strengthens desired behaviors, teaches skills, and nurtures a healthier parent–child bond.

Understanding the difference between these two approaches is not about being permissive or "soft." It is about choosing strategies that actually work—not just today, but in shaping long-term habits, self-control, and resilience.

Why Punishment Falls Short

Punishment is any consequence intended to decrease unwanted behavior. This could be physical (spanking), emotional (shaming), or situational (removing privileges). While punishment can create immediate compliance, it carries hidden costs.

1. Punishment focuses on what not to do, not what to do.
When a child is punished for yelling, they know yelling is wrong—but they don't necessarily learn how to express anger in healthier ways. Without teaching alternatives, punishment leaves a void.

2. Punishment teaches avoidance, not responsibility.
Children often learn to avoid getting caught rather than truly understanding the impact of their actions. For example, a teen punished for lying may simply become better at hiding the truth.

3. Punishment damages trust.

If consequences are harsh or inconsistent, children may see parents as adversaries rather than allies. This undermines the parent–child bond, making discipline less effective over time.

4. Punishment fuels shame instead of growth.

Repeated punishment can make children feel that *they* are bad rather than their behavior being problematic. Shame undermines self-esteem and motivation.

The Science of Positive Reinforcement

Positive reinforcement works by increasing desired behaviors through rewards, praise, or acknowledgment. It focuses not on punishing mistakes but on strengthening what you want to see more of.

B.F. Skinner, the father of operant conditioning, demonstrated that behavior followed by positive reinforcement is more likely to be repeated. This principle is not just theoretical—it has been replicated in countless studies and applied in education, therapy, and parenting with profound success.

For children, reinforcement communicates: *"This behavior works. It brings positive outcomes."* Over time, these repeated experiences build lasting habits and internal motivation.

The Psychology of Motivation

Punishment is based on **extrinsic motivation**—avoiding pain or negative outcomes. Positive reinforcement builds both extrinsic and eventually **intrinsic motivation**. When children experience encouragement, pride, and recognition, they begin to value the behavior itself.

Consider a child who is praised for sharing toys. At first, they may share to earn praise. Over time, they internalize sharing as a positive act, even without external rewards. Punishment rarely produces this shift; it only conditions children to avoid mistakes out of fear.

Real-World Example: Homework Battles

Two families handle homework differently.

Family A punishes: if their child refuses to do homework, they lose screen time. The child completes homework but resents it, viewing schoolwork as a punishment.

Family B uses positive reinforcement: they set up a system where completing homework earns extra playtime or verbal praise. Over time, the child associates effort with positive outcomes, building a sense of accomplishment.

Both families get homework done—but Family B nurtures motivation and responsibility, while Family A breeds compliance mixed with resentment.

Forms of Positive Reinforcement

Positive reinforcement can be applied in various ways:

1. **Verbal Praise:** Simple acknowledgments like, *"I noticed how you helped your sister—that was kind,"* reinforce behaviors children may otherwise overlook.
2. **Physical Affection:** Hugs, high-fives, or a pat on the back signal approval powerfully.
3. **Privileges and Rewards:** Extra playtime, choosing a family activity, or earning tokens toward a goal can motivate consistent effort.
4. **Attention and Presence:** Sometimes the greatest reward is focused parental attention. A parent joining in play or conversation reinforces positive behavior.

Avoiding Common Pitfalls

Positive reinforcement, when misapplied, can backfire.

- **Overpraising:** Constant, generic praise ("Good job!" for everything) dilutes meaning. Praise should be specific: *"I like how you kept trying even when it was hard."*
- **Bribery:** Offering a reward to stop a tantrum reinforces the tantrum itself. Reinforcement should recognize positive behavior, not buy compliance.
- **Overreliance on Material Rewards:** Tangible rewards are effective initially, but they should gradually give way to intrinsic motivation.

The goal is to transition from external rewards to an inner sense of pride, responsibility, and competence.

Positive Reinforcement in Discipline

Positive reinforcement is not about ignoring misbehavior. It is about shifting emphasis. Instead of constantly punishing what children do wrong, parents highlight what they do right. This creates an environment where good behavior is noticed, valued, and repeated.

For example:

- Instead of focusing only on a messy room, notice when your child makes an effort: *"I see you put away your books—that's a great start."*
- Instead of punishing every interruption, reinforce patience: *"Thank you for waiting until I finished speaking. That shows respect."*

Over time, children internalize these cues and begin self-correcting.

When Punishment Is Necessary

While positive reinforcement is more effective overall, there are times when punishment—or more accurately, **logical consequences**—is necessary. If a child throws a toy, the logical consequence may be losing access to the toy for a time. If they refuse to do homework, the natural consequence may be staying in at recess to complete it.

The difference between punishment and logical consequences lies in intent. Punishment seeks to make the child suffer for misbehavior. Logical consequences teach cause-and-effect while maintaining respect. Parents can frame it as: *"Your actions have results. Let's connect them."*

Cultural Shifts in Discipline

Past generations often relied heavily on punishment, viewing it as necessary for instilling discipline. Today, research-driven parenting emphasizes reinforcement, empathy, and natural consequences. This shift does not weaken authority—it strengthens it by aligning discipline with how children actually learn best. Parents who embrace positive reinforcement are not abandoning control; they are replacing fear with influence, and punishment with teaching.

Long-Term Impact of Positive Reinforcement

Children raised in environments rich in positive reinforcement tend to:

- Develop stronger self-esteem, because they feel noticed for their efforts and strengths.
- Build resilience, because encouragement teaches them to keep trying after setbacks.
- Internalize values, because reinforcement links good behavior to positive identity.

- Form healthier relationships, because they learn to use encouragement rather than control in their interactions.

In contrast, children raised primarily with punishment may comply temporarily but often struggle with trust, fear authority, or rebel once external control is removed.

Practical Strategies for Parents

1. **Catch Them Being Good:** Instead of waiting for misbehavior, look for small positive behaviors to reinforce.
2. **Use the 5-to-1 Rule:** Aim for five positive reinforcements for every one correction. This creates an environment where children feel motivated rather than criticized.
3. **Be Consistent:** Reinforcement works best when applied regularly and predictably.
4. **Focus on Effort, Not Just Results:** Praise persistence, problem-solving, and kindness as much as achievements.
5. **Balance Consequences With Reinforcement:** Use logical consequences for misbehavior, but emphasize recognition of good choices.

A Parent's Inner Work

Many parents default to punishment because it mirrors how they were raised. Breaking the cycle requires self-awareness and intentional practice. Ask yourself: *"Am I shaping my child through fear, or through encouragement?"* Shifting from punishment to reinforcement is not about being permissive—it is about being effective.

Final Takeaway

Positive reinforcement and punishment are not equal tools. Punishment may stop behavior temporarily, but it rarely teaches. Positive reinforcement builds skills, motivation, and trust. It rewires the parent–child relationship from conflict to cooperation, creating an environment where children learn not just to avoid mistakes but to pursue strengths. Discipline rooted in reinforcement is not about letting children "get away" with misbehavior—it is about guiding them toward becoming resilient, responsible, and respectful adults.

Creating a Safe Space for Expression

Every child carries emotions too big for their developing minds to handle. Excitement, frustration, sadness, and joy swirl inside them with intensity that often spills out in dramatic ways. For parents, the instinct may be to quiet, redirect, or even dismiss these emotions. *"Stop crying." "Don't be angry." "Calm down right now."* Yet while these responses may silence expression temporarily, they also send a dangerous message: certain feelings are not welcome here.

Children who grow up in environments where emotions are dismissed or punished learn to hide their inner worlds. They may comply outwardly but carry unprocessed feelings that emerge as anxiety, aggression, or disconnection later in life. In contrast, children who are given a safe space to express themselves learn that emotions are not enemies but messengers. They develop emotional intelligence, self-awareness, and resilience. Creating this safe space is not about eliminating boundaries or indulging every feeling. It is about providing a container where emotions can be expressed, understood, and guided constructively.

Why Safe Expression Matters

Psychologists emphasize that emotions serve essential purposes. Anger signals perceived injustice, sadness signals loss, and fear signals danger. These signals are not problems to be erased but data to be understood. When children feel safe expressing emotions, they learn to listen to these signals without being overwhelmed by them.

The alternative is emotional suppression. Studies show that suppressing emotions increases stress, weakens memory, and harms physical health. Children who are told not to cry, not to complain, or not to show anger often internalize the belief that emotions are shameful. They may appear "well-behaved" but struggle silently with emotional regulation. Providing a safe space prevents suppression and teaches constructive coping.

The Link to Emotional Intelligence

Emotional intelligence (EQ) is now recognized as a greater predictor of long-term success than IQ. EQ involves recognizing emotions in oneself and others, managing those emotions effectively, and using them to guide healthy decisions. The foundation of EQ is built in childhood when parents validate feelings and create space for expression.

For example, a child who can say, *"I feel frustrated because I lost the game,"* rather than lashing out in anger demonstrates growing EQ. That capacity begins with adults who make it safe to name and explore emotions without judgment.

What a Safe Space Looks Like

A safe space for expression is not a physical room—it is an atmosphere created by consistent parental responses. Hallmarks include:

- **Nonjudgmental Listening:** Parents hear emotions without ridicule or minimization.
- **Validation of Feelings:** Children are told their feelings are real and understandable, even if their actions must change.
- **Predictable Reactions:** Children know they won't be shamed or rejected for sharing honestly.
- **Guidance, Not Control:** Parents help children channel emotions constructively rather than shutting them down.

In essence, the safe space is the parent–child relationship itself—a relational container where the child feels both secure and guided.

Real-World Example: The Teen Who Withdraws

Consider fourteen-year-old Marcus, who comes home from school sullen and uncommunicative. His father presses for answers, and when Marcus refuses, the father says, *"Fine, be that way. You're always so moody."* Marcus retreats further, feeling misunderstood and unsafe to share.

Now imagine a different response. His father sits beside him and says, *"You seem upset. I'm here if you want to talk. No pressure."* Later, Marcus admits he was embarrassed in class. Because the environment was safe, he chose to share on his own terms. Over time, this repeated experience builds trust: Marcus learns that emotions are not dangerous to reveal.

Common Barriers to Safe Expression

1. **Parental Discomfort with Emotions:** Many parents were raised to hide or suppress feelings and struggle to accept their child's outbursts.
2. **Fear of Disrespect:** Parents sometimes equate emotional expression with defiance, shutting it down to preserve authority.
3. **Overreaction:** When parents panic or get angry at emotions, children learn to conceal them.
4. **Minimization:** Saying, *"It's not a big deal,"* or *"You're overreacting,"* dismisses the child's inner experience.

Recognizing these barriers is the first step toward creating safer emotional environments.

The Role of Boundaries

A safe space does not mean allowing harmful behavior. Children must learn that while all emotions are valid, not all actions are acceptable. For instance:

- "It's okay to feel angry, but it's not okay to hit."
- "It's okay to feel sad, but it's not okay to scream at others."

Boundaries provide the structure that allows safe expression. Without them, children may feel overwhelmed by emotions they cannot control. With them, children learn that feelings can be powerful but manageable.

Cultural Differences in Emotional Expression

Cultures vary widely in how emotions are valued. In some, open expression is encouraged; in others, restraint is seen as maturity. Parents navigating multicultural contexts must balance these values while ensuring children do not internalize shame about emotions. A safe space does not mean unlimited expression but rather respectful acknowledgment tailored to cultural norms.

Practical Strategies for Parents

1. **Name Emotions Together:** Help children build vocabulary. "You look disappointed. Is that how you feel?"
2. **Stay Calm During Outbursts:** Model regulation. A parent's calm presence teaches children that big feelings can be managed.
3. **Validate Before Redirecting:** Start with empathy: "I understand you're frustrated." Then guide: "Let's find another way to show it."
4. **Encourage Expression Through Play or Art:** Younger children may express through drawing, storytelling, or physical activity.
5. **Create Rituals of Sharing:** Use dinner time, bedtime, or car rides as regular opportunities to talk about feelings.
6. **Avoid Judgmental Language:** Replace *"Don't be such a baby"* with *"It's okay to feel sad. Let's talk about it."*

The Long-Term Impact of Safe Expression

Children raised in environments that encourage safe emotional expression:

- Develop higher emotional intelligence.
- Form stronger parent–child bonds based on trust.
- Handle peer conflicts more constructively.
- Experience less anxiety and depression.
- Grow into adults who communicate effectively in relationships.

By contrast, children raised in emotionally unsafe environments may learn to suppress, explode, or numb feelings, often carrying these patterns into adulthood.

A Parent's Inner Work

Creating a safe space requires parents to confront their own relationship with emotions. If you were taught that anger was unacceptable or sadness was weakness, it may feel unnatural to validate those emotions in your child. But breaking that cycle is one of the most powerful gifts you can offer. Ask yourself: *"What messages about emotions did I receive growing up? Do I want to pass those on, or create something new?"*

Final Takeaway

Creating a safe space for expression is not about letting children say or do anything without limits. It is about sending the message: *All your feelings are welcome here. You are safe to be yourself, even when you are sad, angry, or frustrated.* This foundation equips children with emotional intelligence, resilience, and trust. It transforms the parent–child relationship into a secure base from which children can explore the world, confident that home is always a place of understanding and acceptance.

CHAPTER 3

The Role of Boundaries and Structure

Why Children Need Limits to Feel Secure

When parents think of limits, they often imagine conflict: tears at bedtime, arguments about homework, defiance over screen time. Limits are the boundaries that say *"no"* when children desperately want *"yes."* Because of this, many parents feel guilty about enforcing them. They worry that saying no will harm their child's confidence, damage the relationship, or make them seem controlling. Yet research, psychology, and lived experience tell us something profound: children do not just tolerate limits—they need them. Limits provide security, predictability, and structure in a world that otherwise feels overwhelming.

Far from being restrictive cages, limits function as safety rails. They create a defined space where children can explore, take risks, and grow without fear of harm or chaos. A child without limits may appear free but often feels anxious and unanchored. A child with loving, consistent boundaries may resist in the moment but ultimately thrives, knowing the world is predictable and safe.

The Security of Structure

Children are born into a world they do not understand. Rules, routines, and expectations provide order in the midst of confusion. Imagine being dropped into a foreign country with no map, no translator, and no cultural guide. You would feel anxious, disoriented, and unsure of how to behave. That is the daily reality for young children—new experiences, new rules, and limited ability to predict outcomes. Limits, when communicated clearly, function like maps. They tell children: *"This is how the world works. Here are the safe paths to follow."*

Psychologists emphasize that predictability reduces anxiety. When children know what to expect, they can focus energy on learning and play rather than worrying about shifting rules. This is why children often test boundaries—by pushing against them, they are asking: *"Are the rails still there? Can I trust the structure?"* Every time parents enforce limits consistently, they reassure the child: *"The world is safe. Someone is guiding me."*

Limits as an Expression of Love

Many parents hesitate to enforce limits because they fear it will make them less loving. In reality, limits are a profound expression of love. They say: *"I care enough about you to keep you safe, even when you don't like it."* When a parent insists on seatbelts, bedtime routines, or respectful language, they are not being harsh—they are prioritizing the child's well-being.

Children intuitively recognize this over time. Consider the child whose parents never enforce curfews or rules. At first, the child may celebrate freedom, but underneath, they may wonder: *"Does anyone care enough to protect me?"* Contrast this with the child who complains about curfew but later admits feeling safe knowing their parents are watching out for them. Love without limits can feel like neglect. Limits without love can feel like control. The balance of both communicates care.

The Developmental Role of Limits

As children grow, limits serve different purposes.

Toddlers: Limits prevent harm. A toddler exploring the world without boundaries would touch stoves, run into streets, and eat unsafe objects. Limits at this stage are physical safety rails.

Elementary-Age Children: Limits create social learning. Rules about sharing, taking turns, and respecting authority teach children how to function in communities.

Adolescents: Limits foster responsibility. Curfews, expectations about schoolwork, and boundaries around technology help teens learn self-discipline before full independence.

At every stage, limits evolve—but they remain essential. Removing them entirely leaves children developmentally adrift.

The Paradox of Freedom Through Boundaries

It may sound contradictory, but limits actually create freedom. Consider a playground surrounded by a fence. Studies show that children play more confidently and explore further when a fence is present. Without a fence, they cluster near adults, anxious about where the boundaries lie. Similarly, children with clear limits feel freer to explore within the safe space provided.

This paradox extends to adolescence. Teens with clear, consistent rules often experiment less with risky behaviors than those with no limits. The boundaries provide structure, making rebellion less appealing because freedom is already balanced with responsibility.

Why Inconsistent Limits Breed Insecurity

Children are quick to notice inconsistency. If one day bedtime is enforced strictly and the next it is ignored, children feel unsure about expectations. This unpredictability creates anxiety and fuels testing. Inconsistent limits also undermine parental authority—children learn that rules are negotiable based on moods, and they push harder, hoping to catch a moment of leniency.

Consistency, on the other hand, provides stability. Even when children resist, they secretly rely on the predictability of limits. Knowing that bedtime is always bedtime, or that homework always comes before games, removes uncertainty and builds trust.

Real-World Example: Screen Time

Consider two families navigating screen time.

Family A enforces no clear limits. Sometimes screens are allowed during meals, sometimes not. Sometimes hours of gaming go unchecked, sometimes they provoke sudden scolding. The child constantly negotiates, whines, and tests, never sure what the rule really is.

Family B sets a consistent rule: one hour of screens after homework and chores are complete. At first, the child resists. But over time, they stop testing as much because the boundary is predictable. Instead of constant battles, routines settle.

The difference is not stricter rules—it is consistency. Predictable limits reduce conflict and increase security.

The Emotional Side of Limits

Limits do more than regulate behavior; they also regulate emotions. Children who experience consistent boundaries internalize the message: *"Someone stronger than me can handle my feelings."* When parents stay calm and enforce rules firmly, children learn that big emotions do not overwhelm relationships.

For example, when a child screams about bedtime but the parent calmly holds the boundary, the child eventually settles. Over time, they internalize this pattern: emotions can be big, but safety remains intact. Limits become anchors in emotional storms.

Respectful Enforcement of Limits

The way limits are enforced matters as much as the limits themselves. Harsh or authoritarian enforcement breeds fear and resentment. Gentle but firm enforcement communicates both authority and respect. Key strategies include:

- **Explain the Why:** Children are more likely to accept limits when they understand the reasoning. *"We wear helmets because your brain is precious."*
- **Stay Calm:** Emotional escalation undermines authority. Calm firmness models regulation.

- **Acknowledge Feelings:** Validating emotions softens resistance. *"I know you're upset that playtime is over."*
- **Follow Through:** Empty threats erode trust. Limits must be enforced consistently.

Limits as Preparation for Adulthood

Ultimately, limits are not about control but preparation. Life is full of boundaries—traffic laws, workplace expectations, social norms. Children who grow up without limits struggle to adapt to these realities. Those raised with loving, consistent boundaries learn how to navigate structure while maintaining individuality.

Consider college students leaving home for the first time. Those who grew up without limits may lack self-discipline, oversleeping, missing deadlines, or overindulging in freedom. Those who grew up with limits, though they may have resisted at the time, often have stronger internal discipline to manage independence.

When Limits Are Absent

Children raised without boundaries often display:

- **Anxiety:** The unpredictability of life feels overwhelming.
- **Entitlement:** Without boundaries, they expect the world to bend to their desires.
- **Poor Self-Regulation:** They struggle to control impulses without external guidance.
- **Weakened Relationships:** They may clash with authority figures or peers who expect mutual respect.

This is why permissive parenting, while well-intentioned, often backfires. Love without limits creates insecurity rather than confidence.

A Parent's Inner Work

Enforcing limits requires parents to confront their own beliefs about authority. Some fear repeating the harsh discipline they grew up with, so they avoid limits altogether. Others cling to control out of fear of chaos. Finding balance means recognizing that limits are not about dominance but guidance. They are not walls but safety rails.

Parents can ask themselves:

- "Am I avoiding limits out of guilt?"
- "Am I enforcing limits harshly out of fear?"
- "How can I balance firmness with warmth?"

The answers reveal where adjustments may be needed.

Final Takeaway

Children need limits not because they enjoy them, but because limits provide security, structure, and preparation for life. Limits say: *"You are safe. The world has order. I will guide you until you can guide yourself."* Far from restricting growth, loving boundaries give children the confidence to explore, knowing they are anchored in safety. Parenting with limits is not about control—it is about building trust, resilience, and responsibility. In the end, children who grow up with consistent boundaries are not less free—they are more secure, more capable, and more ready for the freedom adulthood requires.

Setting Clear, Consistent Rules

Rules are often misunderstood in parenting. Many parents view them as restrictions—lists of "don'ts" that provoke endless battles. Children see them as arbitrary commands imposed by adults. Yet rules, when set clearly and applied consistently, are not shackles but guides. They define expectations, reduce conflict, and help children internalize discipline. Rules provide children with something invaluable: clarity. And when clarity is paired with consistency, rules stop being sources of rebellion and become tools for security and growth.

Why Rules Matter

Every family has rules, whether spoken or unspoken. Some are explicit: "No hitting." "Homework before screen time." Others are implied: "We don't shout at each other." Children are constantly observing, testing, and interpreting these boundaries. When rules are unclear or inconsistently enforced, confusion reigns. Children don't know what to expect, and parents end up in constant negotiations.

Clear rules simplify family life. They tell children exactly where the boundaries are and what is expected. This reduces power struggles because the rules, not the parent's mood, become the authority. Instead of *"Mom is being strict today,"* the child understands, *"In our family, this is how we do things."*

The Psychology of Clarity

Children thrive on predictability. Their developing brains crave patterns because predictability reduces anxiety. When rules are vague—"Behave yourself" or "Don't make a mess"—children struggle to interpret what behavior is acceptable. Clarity transforms abstract commands into actionable expectations.

Consider the difference:

- Vague: *"Clean your room."*
- Clear: *"Clothes go in the hamper, toys on the shelf, and books on the desk."*

The second gives a roadmap, making success achievable. Clarity removes guesswork, reducing both frustration for the child and nagging for the parent.

The Power of Consistency

Clarity without consistency is fragile. A rule enforced one day but ignored the next invites testing. Children are natural scientists: they test boundaries to see what happens. If ignoring homework sometimes leads to consequences and other times does not, the child learns that pushing is worth the gamble.

Consistency, by contrast, builds trust. Children may resist rules, but they feel secure knowing what to expect. Consistency communicates fairness: rules apply regardless of the parent's mood or the child's persuasion tactics. Over time, this stability becomes internalized. The child doesn't just follow the rule—they learn self-discipline.

Common Pitfalls in Rule-Setting

1. **Too Many Rules:** Overloading children with dozens of rules creates overwhelm and guarantees failure. Fewer, clearer rules are more effective.
2. **Unrealistic Rules:** Rules that ignore developmental stages—like expecting a toddler to sit still for an hour—set children up for failure.
3. **Changing Rules Without Notice:** Shifting expectations breeds insecurity and resentment. Rules should evolve with age, but changes must be explained clearly.
4. **Rules Without Explanation:** Blind commands fuel defiance. Children are more likely to follow rules when they understand the "why."

Real-World Example: Bedtime Battles

Two families approach bedtime differently.

Family A says: *"Go to bed when I tell you."* Sometimes bedtime is at 8:00, sometimes 9:30, depending on the parent's mood. The children argue every night, testing boundaries and negotiating.

Family B sets a clear, consistent rule: bedtime is 8:30 on school nights. The parents explain, *"Your body and brain need rest to learn and play tomorrow."* At first, the children resist, but over time, the predictability reduces conflict. Bedtime is still met with groans, but arguments fade because the rule is consistent.

The difference is not stricter parenting—it is clarity and consistency.

Rules as Family Values in Action

Rules are not just about behavior; they reflect family values. A family that values respect might set rules about speaking kindly. A family that values health might set limits on screen time or sugary snacks. Framing rules as expressions of values helps children understand the bigger picture: *"We do this because it's who we are as a family."*

This shifts rules from arbitrary commands to meaningful practices. Instead of, *"No phones at the table because I said so,"* the parent can say, *"We put phones away at dinner because family time matters here."*

The Role of Communication

Effective rules are co-constructed, not just imposed. While parents must hold authority, involving children in rule-making increases cooperation. Asking, *"What do you think is a fair bedtime?"* or *"How should we handle sharing toys?"* gives children ownership. Even if the parent makes the final decision, the child feels heard.

Family meetings are powerful tools for establishing and revisiting rules. Sitting down together to review what is working, what is not, and what changes may be needed turns rules into shared agreements rather than top-down commands.

Balancing Flexibility and Consistency

Consistency does not mean rigidity. Life requires flexibility—special occasions, travel, or illness may shift routines. The key is distinguishing between exceptions and randomness. If rules bend, children should understand why: *"It's a holiday, so bedtime is later tonight."* This reinforces that rules are consistent, but flexible when circumstances genuinely change.

Discipline Through Rules

Rules also function as proactive discipline. Instead of waiting for misbehavior and reacting, clear rules prevent many conflicts before they start. A rule like, *"We use gentle hands with each other,"* sets expectations that reduce sibling fights. A rule like, *"Homework comes before screens,"* reduces nagging and arguments.

When misbehavior does occur, rules provide a neutral reference point. Instead of, *"You're making me mad,"* parents can say, *"Remember our rule about respecting each other's space."* This shifts discipline from personal confrontation to shared agreement.

Cultural Perspectives on Rules

Different cultures view rules differently. Some emphasize strict obedience, while others prioritize flexibility and negotiation. Neither extreme is universally right or wrong. What matters is whether rules are applied in ways that foster security, fairness, and growth. Parents navigating multicultural environments may need to blend approaches, maintaining authority while also respecting individuality.

Practical Steps for Parents

1. **Identify Core Rules:** Focus on a handful of essential rules aligned with family values.
2. **Make Them Clear:** State rules in simple, specific language children can understand.
3. **Explain the Why:** Connect rules to safety, respect, or family identity.
4. **Enforce Consistently:** Follow through calmly every time. Avoid empty threats.
5. **Review and Adapt:** As children grow, adjust rules together to match new developmental stages.
6. **Model the Rules:** Parents must live by the same standards—children spot hypocrisy instantly.

A Parent's Inner Challenge

Many parents struggle with consistency because of guilt, exhaustion, or fear of conflict. Some bend rules to avoid tears. Others enforce rules harshly, confusing fear with respect. True consistency requires balance: calm firmness rooted in love. Parents can ask themselves:

- "Do my rules reflect my values, or just my frustrations?"
- "Am I following through, or giving in to avoid conflict?"
- "Am I modeling the rules I expect my children to follow?"

These questions help parents set rules that guide rather than control.

Final Takeaway

Clear, consistent rules are not chains—they are compasses. They guide children toward safety, respect, and responsibility. When rules are vague or inconsistent, children feel insecure and push harder. When rules are clear, consistent, and rooted in love, children not only comply but also internalize discipline. In the end, rules are not about control. They are about equipping children to navigate life with confidence, self-regulation, and a strong sense of values.

Using Routines to Reduce Chaos

Every parent has experienced the morning scramble: searching for shoes, rushing to pack lunches, coaxing sleepy children out of bed, and watching the clock tick toward late arrivals. Or the nightly meltdown: endless negotiations about brushing teeth, one more drink of water, and cries of *"I'm not tired yet!"* These chaotic moments are not signs of bad parenting or misbehaving children—they are often signs of missing structure. Routines, far from being boring or rigid, are the secret weapon for reducing stress, preventing conflict, and creating calm.

Children thrive on predictability. Their developing brains crave order in a world that feels unpredictable. When daily activities follow consistent patterns, children feel secure and parents feel less overwhelmed. Routines are not just about saving time; they are about building habits, teaching responsibility, and strengthening family bonds.

Why Routines Work

From a psychological perspective, routines reduce the cognitive load on both children and parents. Each time a child knows what comes next—wake up, eat breakfast, brush teeth—they expend less mental energy deciding or negotiating. This predictability frees their brains for learning, creativity, and play.

For parents, routines reduce decision fatigue. Instead of debating daily when bedtime should be, the rule is already set. Instead of negotiating endlessly about screen time, the routine dictates when it fits. Routines become the neutral authority, removing some of the emotional weight from parenting decisions.

The Neuroscience of Predictability

Children's brains are still developing executive functioning skills—the ability to plan, organize, and regulate behavior. Routines act as external scaffolding, supporting skills they cannot yet manage independently. Repetition strengthens neural pathways. The more a child follows a routine, the more automatic it becomes. Over time, brushing teeth before bed or setting the table before dinner requires less prompting.

Predictability also reduces stress hormones. Uncertainty activates the amygdala, the brain's alarm center. Routines calm this system by signaling safety: *"I know what to expect."* A calmer brain is a more cooperative brain.

Routines vs. Schedules

Parents sometimes confuse routines with rigid schedules. A schedule dictates exact times; a routine emphasizes order and flow. For example:

- Schedule: "Breakfast at 7:15, shoes on at 7:30, car at 7:45."
- Routine: "First we eat breakfast, then we get dressed, then we put on shoes before leaving."

Schedules often break down when life throws surprises—traffic, illness, unexpected events. Routines, by focusing on sequence rather than the clock, provide structure without rigidity. This flexibility makes them sustainable long-term.

The Emotional Benefits of Routines

Routines do more than reduce chaos—they also build emotional security. A child who knows bedtime always includes storytime and a hug feels grounded in predictability and connection. A family who eats dinner together each evening builds a sense of belonging. These rituals communicate: *"You are safe. You are part of something consistent."*

Children with routines often display:

- Lower anxiety, because transitions feel smoother.
- Greater cooperation, because expectations are predictable.
- Stronger self-regulation, because habits become internalized.

Real-World Example: Morning Struggles

Consider two families preparing for school.

Family A has no set routine. Every morning is a negotiation: *"Did you brush your teeth yet? Where's your backpack? Why are you still in pajamas?"* Emotions run high, and the day begins with tension.

Family B follows a simple routine: wake up, get dressed, eat breakfast, brush teeth, pack bag, shoes on, out the door. Each child knows the sequence, reinforced by a visual chart on the wall. There are still occasional protests, but mornings flow with far less chaos.

The difference is not stricter parenting—it is the power of routine.

Building Effective Routines

1. **Start Small:** Focus on one or two problem areas—bedtime or mornings—before overhauling everything.
2. **Make It Visual:** Use charts, checklists, or picture cards for younger children to reinforce steps.
3. **Be Consistent:** Stick with routines long enough for them to become habits.
4. **Involve Children:** Ask for input: *"What should we do first after dinner—homework or play?"* Involvement increases buy-in.
5. **Celebrate Successes:** Reinforce routines with praise: *"You brushed your teeth without reminders—that's responsible."*

Common Routines That Transform Family Life

Morning Routine: Wake up, dress, breakfast, brush teeth, gather belongings.
After-School Routine: Snack, homework, playtime, chores, dinner.
Bedtime Routine: Bath, pajamas, brush teeth, story, lights out.
Mealtime Routine: Set table, eat together, clear dishes.
Screen Time Routine: Screens only after chores/homework, off at a set time.

When these routines are consistent, children know what to expect, and parents spend less time nagging.

Balancing Flexibility with Structure

While consistency is key, flexibility is also important. Special occasions, vacations, or illnesses may disrupt routines. The goal is not rigidity but reliability. Parents can explain changes: *"Usually we have bedtime at 8:30, but tonight we're staying up late for movie night."* This preserves trust by showing that deviations are exceptions, not random chaos.

The Link Between Routines and Independence

Routines also foster independence. A child who follows a bedtime routine with minimal prompting learns self-management. Over time, routines evolve into self-regulation. Instead of parents constantly directing, children internalize habits: *"I brush my teeth before bed because that's what we do."*

Independence grows from predictability. Children who practice routines learn responsibility gradually, preparing them for adolescence and adulthood.

When Routines Are Missing

Families without routines often experience:

- **Frequent Power Struggles:** Every task becomes a negotiation.
- **Heightened Stress:** Parents feel like drill sergeants; children feel overwhelmed.
- **Inconsistent Sleep or Nutrition:** Without structure, children may miss essential health habits.
- **Weak Self-Discipline:** Without practice, children struggle to manage tasks independently.

The absence of routines does not mean parents are failing—it often reflects busyness, exhaustion, or uncertainty about where to start. But even small routines can shift family dynamics dramatically.

Cultural and Personality Differences

Some cultures emphasize communal routines, such as shared meals or prayer times, while others value individual flexibility. Similarly, some children thrive on highly structured routines, while others need looser patterns. Parents can tailor routines to family culture and child temperament while maintaining core consistency. The key is balance: enough structure to reduce chaos, enough flexibility to respect individuality.

A Parent's Inner Challenge

Parents sometimes resist routines because they fear monotony or because their own upbringing lacked structure. Others overcompensate, enforcing rigid schedules that suffocate spontaneity. The challenge is to see routines not as cages but as foundations. They provide stability that frees families to enjoy flexibility without spiraling into chaos.

Parents can ask themselves:

- "Which times of day feel most chaotic in our home?"
- "What one routine would reduce the most stress?"
- "Am I using routines to guide, or schedules to control?"

These questions help parents design routines that support, not restrict.

Final Takeaway

Routines are not about perfection or rigid scheduling—they are about creating predictable rhythms that reduce chaos and build security. They transform power struggles into cooperation, uncertainty into clarity, and stress into stability. By establishing routines, parents give children one of the greatest gifts: the security of knowing what to expect and the confidence to manage themselves. In a world full of unpredictability, routines anchor children in safety, responsibility, and calm.

Balancing Flexibility with Firmness

Parenting often feels like walking a tightrope. On one side is firmness—setting clear rules, enforcing boundaries, and maintaining authority. On the other side is flexibility—listening, adapting, and giving children room to grow. Lean too far toward firmness, and parenting risks becoming rigid, harsh, or authoritarian. Lean too far toward flexibility, and it can slip into permissiveness, inconsistency, or chaos. The art of effective parenting lies not in choosing one side but in balancing both.

Children need the stability of firmness to feel secure, but they also need the adaptability of flexibility to feel understood. This balance prepares them for real life, where rules exist but change is inevitable, where respect matters but negotiation is possible. Finding this middle ground is one of the greatest challenges—and opportunities—of raising children.

Why Firmness Matters

Firmness provides the structure children crave. Without it, the world feels unpredictable, and children are left to guess at boundaries. Firmness communicates: *"I am your guide. I will keep you safe. I will hold limits even when you resist."*

Key benefits of firmness include:

- **Security:** Children feel reassured when limits are clear and consistent.
- **Accountability:** Firmness teaches cause and effect—actions have consequences.
- **Preparation for Society:** Life is full of rules, from school policies to workplace expectations. Firmness at home prepares children to respect external structures.
- **Respect for Authority:** When firmness is fair, children learn to respect boundaries and those who set them.

However, firmness without flexibility can lead to fear, rebellion, or emotional distance.

Why Flexibility Matters

Flexibility acknowledges individuality. It communicates: *"I see you. I hear you. Your needs and feelings matter."* Flexibility teaches adaptability, problem-solving, and collaboration.

Key benefits of flexibility include:

- **Emotional Connection:** Flexibility builds trust and strengthens bonds.
- **Problem-Solving:** Children learn to think creatively when rules can bend thoughtfully.
- **Resilience:** Flexibility teaches that change is part of life and can be navigated successfully.
- **Respect for Self:** Children feel their voices matter, building confidence and autonomy.

However, flexibility without firmness can create entitlement, insecurity, or lack of self-discipline.

The Risks of Imbalance

Too Firm (Authoritarian Parenting):
Children may obey out of fear but often lack internal motivation. They may develop anxiety, low self-esteem, or rebellion when given freedom.

Too Flexible (Permissive Parenting):
Children may feel loved but struggle with boundaries. They may develop entitlement, poor impulse control, or difficulty respecting authority.

The sweet spot is **authoritative parenting**—firm but flexible, high in expectations and high in responsiveness. Research consistently shows this style produces the healthiest outcomes: children who are confident, resilient, responsible, and emotionally secure.

Real-World Example: Curfew Conflicts

Consider two families navigating teenage curfews.

Family A is rigidly firm. Curfew is 9:00 p.m. every night, no exceptions. When their teen asks for a later time for a special school event, the answer is no. The teen sneaks out, resentful and mistrustful.

Family B is overly flexible. Curfew shifts constantly—sometimes 9:00, sometimes midnight, depending on persuasion. The teen learns to manipulate and test limits, pushing further each time.

Family C balances firmness with flexibility. Curfew is 9:00 on school nights, but when the teen asks for an extension for a supervised school event, the parents agree, provided they check in and return by 11:00. The teen feels respected, the parents maintain authority, and trust grows.

The lesson: firmness sets the structure, flexibility adapts it wisely.

The Psychology of Balance

Children interpret parental responses not just as rules but as reflections of love and value. Firmness without warmth can feel like rejection. Flexibility without structure can feel like neglect. Balance communicates both love and guidance: *"I care about your feelings, and I will also protect your well-being with rules."*

Psychologists emphasize that balance strengthens self-regulation. Children internalize both the structure of rules and the adaptability of flexibility, preparing them for adult life where they must navigate expectations while making independent choices.

How to Balance Firmness and Flexibility

1. **Set Core Non-Negotiables:** Identify essential rules tied to safety, respect, and family values. These remain firm.
2. **Allow Flexibility in Non-Essentials:** Offer choices in areas where autonomy can grow—clothing, hobbies, order of chores.
3. **Explain the Why:** Firmness feels less harsh when children understand the reasoning. *"We insist on helmets because your safety matters."*
4. **Invite Dialogue:** Flexibility means hearing children's perspectives, even when rules remain unchanged.
5. **Use Exceptions Thoughtfully:** Break rules occasionally for meaningful reasons—holidays, special achievements—while clarifying why it's an exception.
6. **Stay Consistent in Principles:** Flexibility in details should not undermine the overall structure.

Balancing by Age

Toddlers: Firmness is critical for safety—no running into streets, no touching stoves. Flexibility comes in choices: *"Do you want the red cup or the blue one?"*

Elementary-Age Children: Firmness sets routines—bedtime, homework, chores. Flexibility allows negotiation: *"Do you want to do homework before or after playtime?"*

Adolescents: Firmness defines core rules—curfews, respect, safety. Flexibility involves collaboration: *"Let's talk about how late you can stay for the school dance."*

At every stage, balance adjusts to developmental needs.

Cultural Perspectives on Balance

Different cultures emphasize firmness or flexibility differently. Some value strict obedience; others prize independence. Parents in multicultural contexts may need to blend approaches, ensuring children respect authority while also developing autonomy. Balance provides a bridge: honoring cultural values while preparing children for diverse environments.

A Parent's Inner Challenge

Balancing firmness and flexibility often reflects a parent's own upbringing. Those raised with harsh discipline may overcorrect by becoming too permissive. Those raised with few boundaries may lean toward rigidity to avoid chaos. The challenge is to parent intentionally, not reactively.

Parents can ask themselves:

- "Am I saying no because it's truly important, or because I feel triggered?"
- "Am I giving in because it's best for my child, or because I'm avoiding conflict?"
- "Am I teaching my child resilience, or rescuing them from every discomfort?"

These reflections help parents align their responses with values rather than fears.

Practical Strategies to Practice Balance

1. **Use the "Yes, But" Technique:** Acknowledge feelings while holding boundaries. *"Yes, I know you want to stay up later, but your body needs rest."*
2. **Offer Limited Choices:** Within firm boundaries, give options. *"You must do homework, but you can choose when to start."*
3. **Pause Before Answering:** When asked for exceptions, pause to consider whether flexibility is wise or undermines structure.
4. **Debrief After Exceptions:** If a rule bends, discuss why. *"We stayed up late for the fireworks because it was special. Tomorrow bedtime returns to normal."*
5. **Model Balance in Your Life:** Show how you respect rules but adapt to circumstances—like following traffic laws but slowing down in rain for safety.

The Long-Term Impact

Children raised with balanced firmness and flexibility:

- Respect authority without fear.
- Develop independence without entitlement.
- Handle change with resilience.
- Build strong self-discipline alongside empathy.

In contrast, children raised with only firmness may obey but lack confidence, while those raised with only flexibility may feel loved but lack structure. Balance produces the healthiest blend: confidence anchored in security.

Final Takeaway

Parenting is not about choosing firmness or flexibility—it is about weaving both together. Firmness provides the rails of safety and consistency. Flexibility provides the cushions of empathy and adaptability. Together, they create a path where children feel secure, respected, and prepared for real life. When parents strike this balance, they raise children who are not only disciplined but also adaptable, not only respectful but also independent.

Preventing Power Struggles Before They Begin

Few experiences drain parents more than constant power struggles. A simple request—*"Put on your shoes"*—spirals into negotiations, whining, or outright refusal. What should be a five-minute task becomes a thirty-minute battle. These struggles often leave both child and parent frustrated, angry, and disconnected. But what if many of these conflicts could be prevented before they even start?

Power struggles are not inevitable. They arise when children feel a clash between their need for autonomy and the boundaries set by adults. By understanding the roots of these struggles and proactively addressing them, parents can reduce conflict dramatically. Preventing power struggles is not about giving in to children's demands, nor is it about exerting relentless control. It is about creating an environment where cooperation feels natural and battles are unnecessary.

Why Power Struggles Happen

Children, like adults, have an innate need for autonomy. Psychologists Edward Deci and Richard Ryan describe autonomy as a core psychological need, essential for motivation and well-being. When children feel their choices are ignored or their independence is threatened, they resist. A parent insisting, *"Do it because I said so,"* often triggers defiance not because the task is unreasonable but because the child's autonomy feels dismissed.

Another factor is predictability. When rules or expectations shift, children test boundaries to regain clarity. Inconsistent enforcement makes them push harder, wondering: *"Will the rule hold this time?"*

Finally, power struggles often escalate because both parent and child enter "fight mode." The child resists, the parent tightens control, and the cycle feeds itself until both are entrenched. Preventing power struggles means breaking this cycle before it starts.

The Role of Choice

One of the simplest ways to prevent power struggles is by offering choices within boundaries. Instead of, *"Put on your shoes now,"* say, *"Do you want to wear the red shoes or the blue ones?"* The task still gets done, but the child feels empowered.

Choices satisfy autonomy without sacrificing structure. They signal: *"I respect your voice, but I'm guiding the outcome."* For younger children, choices should be limited and clear. For older children, they can involve more meaningful input, such as negotiating chore schedules or selecting extracurricular activities.

Clear Expectations Reduce Resistance

Unclear or vague expectations are breeding grounds for conflict. A rule like, *"Behave yourself,"* leaves room for debate. Specific expectations—*"Inside voices at the library," "Homework before screens,"*—eliminate ambiguity.

Posting family rules, using visual charts for routines, and reminding children in advance reduce testing. When children know exactly what is expected, they are less likely to resist.

Timing Matters

Power struggles often erupt when children are tired, hungry, or overstimulated. Asking a child to clean their room right before dinner or insisting on chores late at night almost guarantees conflict. Preventing struggles means anticipating vulnerable times and adjusting expectations.

This does not mean eliminating rules during difficult moments, but rather choosing battles wisely. A well-timed reminder in the morning may work better than a late-night demand. Parents who attune to timing prevent unnecessary resistance.

Staying Calm as Prevention

Children often mirror parents' emotional states. A parent who issues commands in frustration—*"I've told you a hundred times!"*—invites defiance. A calm tone, eye contact, and steady presence reduce escalation before it starts.

Calmness is not weakness; it is authority without aggression. Neuroscience shows that children's nervous systems regulate in response to caregivers' regulation. By staying calm, parents prevent children's emotions from spiraling into battles.

The Power of Predictable Routines

Routines prevent power struggles by removing negotiation. If a child knows homework always comes before screens, the parent is not the bad guy enforcing the rule—the routine is. Instead of debating daily, the structure becomes the authority.

Routines also reduce decision fatigue. Children no longer wonder, *"Do I have to brush my teeth tonight?"* because the answer is always yes. Predictability makes compliance easier and arguments unnecessary.

Respectful Communication

Language matters. Demands framed harshly provoke resistance; requests framed respectfully invite cooperation. Compare:

- *"Stop being lazy and clean your room!"*
- *"It's time to clean your room. Do you want to start with toys or clothes?"*

The second approach communicates respect, provides choice, and reduces defensiveness. Respectful communication does not weaken authority—it strengthens it by modeling how conflicts can be resolved without hostility.

Real-World Example: Grocery Store Meltdowns

Consider a parent shopping with their four-year-old. The child demands candy at checkout. The parent, embarrassed, says sharply, *"No! Stop asking!"* The child screams louder. A battle ensues.

Now imagine a preventive approach. Before entering the store, the parent explains: *"Today we're buying food for dinner. You may choose one healthy snack."* The child's need for choice is met, the parent's boundary is clear, and the checkout line passes without conflict. Prevention begins not at checkout but before the store.

Teaching Emotional Vocabulary

Sometimes power struggles erupt because children lack words for their feelings. Instead of saying, *"I'm tired,"* they resist bedtime. Instead of saying, *"I'm disappointed,"* they throw a tantrum. Teaching emotional vocabulary—sad, frustrated, excited—gives children alternatives to defiance.

Parents can model this: *"I can see you're frustrated about leaving the park. It's hard to stop playing when you're having fun."* Naming feelings validates the child and prevents escalation.

Knowing When to Step Back

Not every issue deserves a battle. Parents who fight every small resistance drain energy and strain relationships. Preventing power struggles means distinguishing between essential and negotiable. Safety, respect, and health are non-negotiable. Clothing choices, toy organization, or minor preferences often allow for flexibility.

Stepping back does not mean surrender—it means saving energy for the battles that truly matter.

Avoiding Empty Threats

Power struggles escalate when parents issue threats they cannot enforce. *"If you don't stop, we're never coming back to the park again!"* Such statements invite testing and erode credibility. Prevention means setting limits you can and will enforce. Children respect boundaries that are realistic and consistent.

When Prevention Fails

No strategy prevents every conflict. Children are learning, testing, and developing autonomy. Even with the best prevention, power struggles will sometimes arise. In those moments, staying calm, holding firm boundaries, and reconnecting afterward matter most.

But the more parents invest in prevention, the fewer battles they face.

The Long-Term Benefits of Prevention

When parents consistently prevent unnecessary power struggles, children learn cooperation without resentment. They internalize that authority is fair, respectful, and predictable. Over time, this reduces resistance, builds trust, and strengthens the parent–child bond.

Children raised in environments where battles are minimized develop:

- Stronger self-regulation, because they practice cooperation instead of constant defiance.
- Greater respect for authority, because rules feel consistent and fair.
- Better problem-solving skills, because negotiation is modeled constructively.
- Healthier relationships, because respect and collaboration are the norm.

A Parent's Inner Challenge

Preventing power struggles often requires parents to confront their own triggers. Many grew up in homes where authority was unquestioned, and resistance feels threatening. Others grew up with little structure and fear being too strict. Recognizing these patterns helps parents respond intentionally rather than reactively.

Questions to reflect on include:

- "Am I enforcing this because it matters, or because I feel challenged?"
- "Am I giving in because it's best for my child, or because I want to avoid conflict?"
- "How can I set boundaries that are both firm and respectful?"

These reflections shift parenting from reaction to strategy.

Final Takeaway

Power struggles are not signs of failure—they are signals. They reveal children's need for autonomy, clarity, and respect. By preventing battles before they begin—through choices, routines, calm communication, and clear expectations—parents reduce conflict dramatically. The goal is not to win every argument but to create an environment where arguments are rarely necessary. Preventing power struggles is not about control; it is about guidance. It transforms daily life from constant battles into cooperative growth, freeing both parent and child to focus on connection, learning, and joy.

CHAPTER 4

Effective Communication Strategies

Listening Beyond the Tantrum

Few moments test a parent's patience like a child in the throes of a tantrum. Whether it's a toddler screaming in the grocery store, a seven-year-old throwing toys after losing a game, or a teenager slamming doors in frustration, the instinctive reaction is often to stop the noise, restore order, and move on. But beneath every tantrum lies something deeper: a message. Children tantrum not because they are "bad" or "spoiled," but because they are overwhelmed, frustrated, or unable to communicate what they truly feel. The challenge for parents is to listen not just to the outburst but to the meaning behind it.

Listening beyond the tantrum is not about indulging every demand or allowing chaos to reign. It is about recognizing that behavior is communication. When parents shift from seeing tantrums as disobedience to seeing them as signals, they move from reacting to responding, from controlling to teaching, and from conflict to connection.

Why Children Tantrum

Tantrums happen when emotions overwhelm a child's ability to cope. This is especially common because the brain systems for emotional regulation develop much later than the systems for emotional reactivity. In simple terms, children feel big emotions long before they can manage them.

Key triggers for tantrums include:

- **Frustration:** A toy doesn't work, homework feels impossible, or a game is lost.
- **Transitions:** Shifting from play to bedtime, or leaving a fun activity, often sparks resistance.
- **Overstimulation:** Noise, crowds, or too many demands overwhelm the nervous system.

- **Unmet Needs:** Hunger, fatigue, or lack of attention lower tolerance for frustration.
- **Blocked Autonomy:** When children feel powerless, they may explode in protest.

Recognizing these triggers helps parents anticipate tantrums and respond with empathy rather than anger.

The Brain in a Tantrum

During a tantrum, a child's brain is in survival mode. The amygdala—the brain's alarm center—is fully activated, flooding the body with stress hormones. The prefrontal cortex—the rational, problem-solving part of the brain—is offline. This means children literally cannot reason, negotiate, or listen until they calm down.

Parents who try to explain or argue mid-tantrum often feel ignored, but it's not defiance—it's biology. Listening beyond the tantrum requires patience: first help the child regulate, then teach.

The Difference Between Hearing and Listening

Hearing a tantrum means focusing on the noise: the crying, screaming, or yelling. Listening means asking: *"What is my child trying to tell me through this outburst?"*

For example:

- A toddler screaming for a cookie may be expressing hunger, tiredness, or the need for comfort.
- A child throwing a backpack after school may be expressing shame over a difficult test.
- A teen shouting "Leave me alone!" may be expressing fear of failure or need for independence.

The behavior is the surface. The feeling is the depth. True listening means looking beneath the surface.

Responding with Presence

Listening beyond the tantrum begins with presence. Children in emotional overload need to know their parent is steady, calm, and available. This does not mean agreeing with demands, but it does mean staying connected.

A parent who yells back escalates the storm. A parent who withdraws entirely leaves the child alone with emotions too big to handle. Presence is the middle path: calm, firm, empathetic. Sitting nearby, offering a gentle touch if welcomed, or simply waiting quietly signals: *"I'm here. You're safe. We'll get through this together."*

The Power of Validation

Validation is one of the most powerful tools in de-escalating tantrums. It communicates: *"Your feelings make sense, even if your behavior must change."*

Examples include:

- "I can see you're really frustrated that your toy broke."
- "It's disappointing to leave the park when you were having fun."
- "I know you're angry about the homework—it feels hard right now."

Validation does not mean giving in. It means acknowledging the emotion so the child feels seen. Once emotions are validated, children calm faster and are more open to guidance.

Real-World Example: The Grocery Store Meltdown

Imagine a toddler screaming for candy at the checkout line. A reactive parent snaps: *"Stop it right now! You're embarrassing me!"* The child screams louder. The battle intensifies.

Now imagine a parent kneeling down and saying: *"I know you really want candy. It looks yummy, doesn't it? But today we're buying food for dinner. You can help me choose apples instead."* The child may still cry, but the intensity decreases. They feel acknowledged, not dismissed. The meltdown ends sooner, and trust is preserved.

Teaching After the Tantrum

The moment for teaching is not during the outburst but after calm has returned. Once the child is regulated, parents can reflect together:

- "Next time you're frustrated, what could you do instead of yelling?"
- "When you feel upset, how can you let me know in words?"
- "What can we do to make transitions easier next time?"

These conversations transform tantrums into lessons, teaching children emotional vocabulary, problem-solving, and self-control.

Preventing Future Tantrums

Listening beyond tantrums also means noticing patterns and preventing triggers when possible.

- **Anticipate Transitions:** Give warnings before leaving fun activities. *"Five more minutes at the park, then we go."*
- **Meet Physical Needs:** Ensure snacks, rest, and downtime to reduce vulnerability.
- **Offer Choices:** Provide autonomy within limits. *"Do you want to brush your teeth before or after pajamas?"*
- **Practice Coping Tools:** Teach deep breathing, squeezing a stress ball, or using words like "I'm mad."

Prevention does not eliminate all tantrums, but it reduces frequency and intensity.

When to Worry

Occasional tantrums are developmentally normal. However, frequent, intense, or destructive outbursts may signal deeper issues such as anxiety, ADHD, or trauma. If tantrums consistently overwhelm the child and family, professional support can provide strategies and insight. Seeking help is not failure—it is proactive care.

The Parent's Inner Work

Listening beyond the tantrum also requires parents to manage their own triggers. Many adults grew up in households where tantrums were met with punishment or shame. Their instinct may be to silence rather than listen. Breaking this cycle requires self-awareness. Parents can ask themselves:

- "What emotions do my child's tantrums trigger in me?"
- "Am I reacting from frustration, or responding with empathy?"
- "What message do I want my child to remember after this moment?"

By regulating themselves, parents model the very skills they hope to teach.

The Long-Term Impact

Children who are listened to—even in their worst moments— develop resilience and emotional intelligence. They learn that emotions are manageable, that their voices matter, and that relationships can withstand conflict. Over time, tantrums decrease because children gain tools to express themselves constructively.

Children who are dismissed or punished harshly for tantrums, however, may learn to suppress emotions, lash out aggressively, or seek attention through rebellion. Listening does not mean permissiveness; it means guiding children to transform overwhelming feelings into constructive expression.

Final Takeaway

Tantrums are not just noise to be silenced—they are messages to be understood. Listening beyond the tantrum means recognizing behavior as communication, validating emotions, and guiding children toward healthier coping. It requires calm presence, empathy, and patience. But the reward is profound: fewer battles, deeper trust, and children who grow into emotionally intelligent, resilient adults. When parents learn to listen beyond the tantrum, they discover that the storm is not the end of connection—it is the doorway to it.

Choosing Words That Defuse Conflict

Words are powerful. They can ignite battles or dissolve them, wound or heal, shame or strengthen. In parenting, words often determine whether a conflict escalates into a shouting match or softens into connection. Children are acutely sensitive to language; they hear not only the content of what parents say but also the tone, intent, and emotion behind it. Choosing words carefully is not about being overly cautious or walking on eggshells—it is about recognizing that language shapes behavior, relationships, and self-image.

When parents consistently use words that defuse rather than inflame conflict, they teach children emotional regulation, model respectful communication, and reduce unnecessary power struggles. The result is not permissiveness but authority expressed with calm and clarity.

Why Words Matter in Conflict

Children live in a world where adults hold most of the power. They have less control over their time, choices, and environment. Words are often the primary tools parents use to exercise authority. Harsh or careless words can make children feel small, powerless, or ashamed. Respectful, thoughtful words communicate authority without humiliation.

Research in developmental psychology shows that children internalize the words parents use. A child repeatedly called "lazy" may begin to see themselves as incapable. A child who hears, "I know you can do this" internalizes competence and confidence. Words don't just shape moments of conflict—they shape identities.

The Escalating Power of Negative Language

Parents often use negative language unintentionally, especially under stress. Common phrases include:

- "Why can't you ever listen?"
- "You're acting like a baby."
- "If you don't stop, you'll regret it."
- "What's wrong with you?"

These phrases escalate conflict by attacking character rather than addressing behavior. They trigger defensiveness, shame, or rebellion. The child focuses less on correcting behavior and more on protecting their sense of worth.

Reframing Language: Behavior vs. Identity

One key to defusing conflict is separating behavior from identity. Instead of labeling the child, describe the behavior:

- Instead of: "You're so messy."
- Say: "Your toys are scattered. Let's put them back."

- Instead of: "You're so rude."
- Say: "That comment was unkind. Let's try again respectfully."

This reframing preserves dignity while still holding accountability. The child hears: *"I made a mistake,"* rather than, *"I am a mistake."*

The Science of Calming Language

Neuroscience shows that certain words and tones activate the child's stress response, while others calm it. Harsh commands or threats activate the amygdala, triggering fight-or-flight responses. Calm, empathetic language engages the prefrontal cortex, allowing rational thinking to return.

Phrases that calm include:

- "I can see you're upset."
- "Let's take a breath together."
- "We'll figure this out."
- "You're safe. I'm here."

These words reassure the nervous system, making cooperation possible.

Real-World Example: Homework Resistance

Consider a parent facing nightly homework battles.

Scenario A: The parent says, *"You're so lazy. Why can't you just sit down and do it?"* The child feels attacked, resists harder, and the battle escalates.

Scenario B: The parent says, *"I know homework feels frustrating. Let's start with just one problem together."* The child feels understood, tension eases, and progress begins.

The task remains the same, but the words shift the outcome dramatically.

Choosing Authority Without Aggression

Some parents fear that softening language weakens authority. In reality, calm authority is stronger than aggressive control. Children respect firmness expressed with respect more than they respect shouting. Words that defuse conflict balance empathy with boundaries:

- "I hear that you don't want to clean up. It's still time to do it."
- "I know you're angry, but hitting is not okay. Let's find another way."

These statements acknowledge feelings while upholding limits. The message is clear: emotions are valid, but boundaries remain firm.

Avoiding Triggers: Words That Inflame

Certain phrases almost guarantee escalation. These include:

- **Always/Never Statements:** "You always argue." "You never listen." These exaggerations breed defensiveness.
- **Comparisons:** "Why can't you be like your sister?" Comparisons fuel resentment and insecurity.
- **Sarcasm:** Children may not understand sarcasm, but they feel its sting.
- **Empty Threats:** "Do that again and you'll never watch TV again!" Unrealistic consequences erode credibility.

Replacing these with specific, respectful language prevents unnecessary battles.

Using Positive Framing

Positive language focuses on what to do rather than what not to do. Compare:

- Negative: "Stop running in the house!"
- Positive: "Walk inside so we stay safe."
- Negative: "Don't interrupt me!"
- Positive: "Wait until I finish, then it's your turn."

Positive framing guides behavior constructively while avoiding the resistance triggered by constant "don'ts."

The Role of Tone and Body Language

Words alone are not enough; tone and body language communicate just as powerfully. A calm tone, eye contact, and open posture reinforce respect. A raised voice, finger-pointing, or looming over a child may trigger fear or defiance, regardless of the words used.

For example, saying "I need you to pick up your toys" with a calm tone communicates authority. The same words shouted in anger communicate hostility. Tone transforms meaning.

Teaching Through Modeling

Children learn how to use words in conflict by observing parents. A parent who apologizes, rephrases, or chooses calm words models conflict resolution. Saying, *"I was frustrated and spoke harshly. Let me try again,"* teaches humility and respect. Over time, children absorb these skills, using them in peer relationships and future partnerships.

Practical Strategies for Parents

1. **Pause Before Speaking:** A deep breath can prevent reactive words.
2. **Use "I" Statements:** *"I need you to speak calmly so I can understand,"* rather than *"You're so loud."*
3. **Offer Empathy First:** Acknowledge feelings before correcting behavior.
4. **Be Specific:** Replace vague commands with clear instructions. *"Please put the blocks in the bin."*
5. **Lower Your Voice:** Speaking softly often compels children to listen more closely.
6. **Practice Repair:** If harsh words slip out, model accountability by apologizing.

A Parent's Inner Work

Choosing words that defuse conflict requires self-awareness. Parents under stress may revert to patterns from their own upbringing— harsh words, threats, or sarcasm. Reflecting on these patterns helps break the cycle. Ask yourself:

- "What words do I use most often in conflict?"
- "Do my words build trust or erode it?"
- "What message about themselves do my children hear through my language?"

By practicing intentional speech, parents create homes where respect and cooperation replace fear and defiance.

The Long-Term Impact

Children raised with words that defuse conflict learn to:

- Regulate emotions more effectively.
- Use respectful communication in peer and adult relationships.

- Internalize discipline without shame.
- Develop higher self-esteem and confidence.

By contrast, children raised with harsh, shaming language may obey temporarily but often struggle with resentment, low self-worth, or difficulty managing conflict constructively.

Final Takeaway

Words can inflame conflict or extinguish it. They can wound identities or build resilience. Choosing words that defuse conflict does not mean avoiding correction—it means delivering it with clarity, respect, and calm authority. When parents master this skill, they transform everyday struggles into opportunities for growth. They raise children who not only listen but also learn, not only obey but also respect, and not only follow rules but also develop character. In the end, the language parents choose becomes the language children use—with themselves, with others, and with the world.

Non-Verbal Signals Kids Pick Up On

Parents often focus on the words they use with their children, carefully choosing phrases that encourage cooperation, teach lessons, or express love. Yet research shows that the majority of human communication is non-verbal. Children, especially, are attuned to the subtle cues of tone, posture, facial expressions, and gestures. They may not always understand complex words, but they read bodies and voices with remarkable accuracy.

This means that parents are always communicating—sometimes even more powerfully through what they don't say than through what they do. A sigh of frustration, a roll of the eyes, or crossed arms can undermine spoken words, while a gentle smile, open posture, or calm tone can reinforce them. Recognizing and mastering non-verbal signals allows parents to align their actions with their intentions, sending messages of security, respect, and love.

Why Non-Verbal Signals Matter

Children are born without advanced language skills but with strong emotional radar. From infancy, babies detect tone, rhythm, and expression. They respond more to the warmth in a caregiver's voice or the tension in their body than to the actual words spoken.

As children grow, this sensitivity continues. They may hear a parent say, *"I'm not angry,"* but if the parent's jaw is clenched and voice is sharp, the child trusts the body language more than the words. When verbal and non-verbal messages clash, children believe the non-verbal.

This is why non-verbal communication is crucial. It shapes not only how children respond in the moment but also how they develop trust, self-esteem, and emotional intelligence.

The Science Behind Non-Verbal Communication

Psychologists note that up to 70% of communication is non-verbal. This includes:

- **Facial Expressions:** Joy, disappointment, anger, and love are conveyed instantly without words.
- **Tone of Voice:** Calmness, sarcasm, frustration, and warmth are communicated in how something is said, not just what is said.
- **Body Language:** Posture, gestures, and movement signal authority, openness, or tension.
- **Touch:** A gentle pat, a hug, or a firm hand can comfort or correct more effectively than words.

Neuroscience also reveals that children's mirror neurons—brain cells that fire when observing others—make them especially attuned to parents' emotions. When a parent expresses calm through body language, the child's nervous system often mirrors that calm. When a parent radiates tension, the child absorbs it.

Common Non-Verbal Messages Parents Send

Parents may unintentionally send signals that escalate conflict or weaken authority. Some common examples include:

- **Eye-Rolling or Sarcasm:** Signals disrespect, even if the words are neutral.
- **Raised Voice and Pointing Finger:** Communicates threat, often triggering defensiveness.
- **Crossed Arms:** Suggests closed-off or punitive stance, even without harsh words.
- **Avoiding Eye Contact:** Signals disinterest or disconnection.

On the other hand, intentional non-verbal cues can strengthen communication:

- **Gentle Eye Contact:** Shows attention and respect.
- **Kneeling to Eye Level:** Reduces intimidation and signals connection.
- **Open Posture:** Communicates availability and calm.
- **Soft Touch:** Reinforces warmth and reassurance.

Real-World Example: The Contradiction

A mother tells her child, *"I'm listening, tell me what happened at school."* But while the child speaks, the mother checks her phone, nodding absently. The words say interest, but the body language says distraction. The child senses the truth and stops talking.

Now imagine the same mother putting the phone aside, turning fully toward the child, leaning forward slightly, and making eye contact. Even without words, the child feels valued. The message is not only heard but believed.

The Role of Tone

Tone often carries more weight than content. A calm "Stop" communicates authority; a shouted "STOP!" may trigger fear or defiance. Tone also conveys emotional states children cannot yet name. A sarcastic remark may confuse younger children, while a harsh tone may wound older ones even when the words seem mild.

Parents who modulate tone—keeping it calm, steady, and respectful—create an environment where children are more likely to listen and less likely to resist.

Non-Verbal Signals in Discipline

Discipline is often more effective when parents rely on non-verbal signals rather than escalating words. A steady look, a pause, or walking over to a child communicates seriousness without yelling. This avoids power struggles fueled by verbal sparring.

For example, a teacher managing a noisy classroom often regains attention not by shouting but by standing silently with presence until the room quiets. Parents can use similar strategies at home—body language that commands respect without aggression.

Non-Verbal Reassurance

Equally important are the non-verbal signals of comfort. A hug after discipline, a smile across the dinner table, or a reassuring hand on the shoulder communicates love more effectively than words alone. These small gestures anchor children in security: *"Even when I make mistakes, I am loved."*

Cultural Differences in Non-Verbal Communication

Non-verbal cues vary across cultures. In some cultures, direct eye contact signals respect; in others, it may be seen as defiance. Physical touch may be common in some families, rare in others. Parents must be mindful of cultural contexts while ensuring that children still receive consistent signals of love, attention, and authority.

Teaching Children Non-Verbal Awareness

By being intentional with their own non-verbal signals, parents also teach children to interpret and use them. This builds social awareness, empathy, and communication skills. For example, narrating body language can help: *"I crossed my arms because I was frustrated,"* or *"Did you see how your friend smiled when you shared? That means she felt happy."*

Over time, children become more skilled at reading others' emotions and managing their own non-verbal cues—a key part of emotional intelligence.

Practical Strategies for Parents

1. **Align Words and Actions:** Ensure body language matches the message. Saying "I'm not mad" while glaring confuses children.
2. **Practice Neutral Presence:** Instead of escalating, use calm posture and tone to assert authority.
3. **Use Eye Level:** Kneel or sit to match the child's height during correction or connection.
4. **Pause Before Responding:** A moment of silence, combined with steady eye contact, often carries more weight than immediate words.
5. **Be Aware of Micro-Expressions:** Even small signs of frustration—sighs, rolled eyes—are noticed by children.

6. **Use Positive Touch:** Gentle physical reassurance strengthens connection.

A Parent's Inner Challenge

Non-verbal signals are often unconscious, shaped by stress, fatigue, or upbringing. A parent who grew up in a household of shouting may unintentionally default to aggressive tones or harsh gestures. Becoming aware of these habits is the first step to change. Ask yourself:

- "What do my body and tone communicate when I'm frustrated?"
- "Do my non-verbal signals align with my words?"
- "What signals do I want my children to remember most?"

By aligning body, tone, and words, parents create homes of clarity and trust.

The Long-Term Impact

Children raised in environments where non-verbal signals reinforce respect and love develop:

- Stronger trust in authority, because words and actions match.
- Higher emotional intelligence, because they learn to read and respond to subtle cues.
- Greater resilience, because non-verbal reassurance anchors them in love.
- Better communication skills, because they model respectful tone and posture.

Children raised with conflicting or hostile non-verbal signals may feel confused, mistrustful, or insecure. They may say, *"I never knew what my parent really meant,"* or struggle with reading cues in their own relationships.

Final Takeaway

Children may not remember every word parents say, but they will always remember how those words felt. Non-verbal signals—tone, posture, touch, and expression—carry messages that shape identity and trust. By becoming intentional about these cues, parents can defuse conflict, reinforce authority, and build lasting connection. Listening is important, but so is *showing*. When words and actions align, children feel safe, respected, and deeply loved.

Teaching Emotional Vocabulary

Imagine a child screaming in frustration because their toy broke, or a teenager slamming their bedroom door after school. Often, beneath the noise is an emotion too big to express and too complex to name. Children act out not because they want to misbehave but because they lack the words to explain what they feel. Emotional vocabulary—the ability to identify and name emotions—is a cornerstone of emotional intelligence. When children can put words to feelings, they gain control over them. Without this skill, emotions erupt through tantrums, withdrawal, or aggression.

Teaching emotional vocabulary is one of the most powerful gifts parents can give. It equips children to understand themselves, communicate effectively, and navigate relationships with empathy and confidence.

Why Emotional Vocabulary Matters

Words shape experience. A child who can say, *"I feel frustrated"* is better equipped to handle that feeling than one who only knows how to cry, yell, or lash out. Psychologists call this "emotional granularity"—the ability to distinguish between emotions. Research by Lisa Feldman Barrett shows that children with higher emotional granularity manage stress better, recover from setbacks more quickly, and display stronger social skills.

Without emotional vocabulary, children often default to extremes—everything is either "good" or "bad," "happy" or "mad." Nuanced language allows for more precise self-understanding: *"I feel disappointed, not furious."* This precision reduces emotional overwhelm and guides better coping strategies.

The Link Between Words and Regulation

The act of labeling emotions engages the brain's prefrontal cortex, calming the amygdala—the emotional alarm system. This process, sometimes called "name it to tame it" (coined by psychologist Daniel Siegel), explains why naming feelings reduces their intensity. When a child says, *"I'm nervous about my test,"* the nervousness feels less consuming than when it is expressed only as stomach aches or refusal to study.

Teaching emotional vocabulary, then, is not just about language. It is about regulation. It gives children tools to manage emotions instead of being managed by them.

Starting Early: Building a Foundation

Even toddlers can learn basic emotional words. At first, these may include simple categories: happy, sad, mad, scared. Parents can model by narrating feelings in real time:

- "You look sad because your toy broke."
- "You're smiling—you feel happy we're playing."

As language skills grow, vocabulary expands: frustrated, disappointed, nervous, excited, proud. Each new word provides a tool for self-expression.

Real-World Example: The After-School Meltdown

Consider a seven-year-old who bursts into tears after school. Asked what's wrong, they shrug or yell, *"I don't know!"* Without words, the emotion remains overwhelming.

Now imagine the parent saying: *"It looks like you're frustrated. Did something at school feel unfair?"* The child nods, finally able to connect the word to the feeling. By naming frustration, the parent gives the child power to understand and process it.

Expanding the Emotional Dictionary

Parents can build emotional vocabulary gradually:

- **Introduce New Words in Context:** "You seem disappointed we can't go to the park today."
- **Use Stories and Books:** Pause to ask, "How do you think this character feels? What word describes it?"
- **Play Emotion Games:** Use flashcards with faces or act out emotions to practice labeling.
- **Encourage Self-Expression:** Ask, "What word fits how you feel right now?"

Over time, children move beyond basic emotions to more complex states: overwhelmed, anxious, relieved, grateful. This deepens their emotional intelligence.

Teaching the Difference Between Emotions and Actions

One crucial lesson is separating feelings from behaviors. All feelings are acceptable; not all actions are. For example:

- "It's okay to feel angry. It's not okay to hit."
- "You can feel frustrated. You cannot throw your toys."

This distinction prevents shame while teaching responsibility. Children learn that emotions are messages, not commands.

The Role of Parents as Emotional Translators

Parents often serve as emotional translators in early years. When a toddler screams after a block tower falls, the parent might say: *"You're frustrated because it fell after you worked hard."* Over time, the child begins to supply the words themselves. The parent gradually shifts from translator to coach, prompting but not providing every answer: *"You look upset. Can you tell me the word for how you feel?"*

Emotional Vocabulary Across Ages

Toddlers: Focus on basic words (happy, sad, mad, scared). Use simple sentences and facial expressions.

Elementary-Age Children: Expand vocabulary (frustrated, nervous, proud, disappointed). Introduce the idea of mixed feelings: *"You feel nervous and excited about the play."*

Adolescents: Encourage nuance and complexity (insecure, overwhelmed, hopeful, discouraged). Acknowledge layered emotions: *"It sounds like you're both relieved the test is over and worried about the grade."*

Each stage builds on the last, preparing children for adult-level emotional intelligence.

Cultural Perspectives on Emotional Expression

Cultures differ in how emotions are expressed and labeled. Some emphasize emotional restraint; others encourage openness. Teaching emotional vocabulary does not mean forcing children into one cultural mold. It means giving them tools to navigate emotions in ways that fit both family values and broader society. Parents can model respect for cultural differences while still validating emotional experiences.

Practical Strategies for Teaching Emotional Vocabulary

1. **Model Aloud:** Share your feelings openly. *"I'm frustrated that the traffic is slow, but I'm taking deep breaths."*
2. **Use Visual Aids:** Emotion charts or wheels help children connect words with faces.
3. **Practice Daily Check-Ins:** Ask, "How are you feeling?" during dinner or bedtime.
4. **Praise Expression:** Acknowledge when children use words: *"Thank you for telling me you're nervous instead of yelling."*
5. **Encourage Journaling:** For older children, writing feelings builds awareness and vocabulary.
6. **Correct Gently:** If a child says "mad" when they mean "disappointed," guide them toward the more accurate word.

When Children Resist

Some children, especially older ones, may resist naming emotions, seeing it as unnecessary or uncomfortable. In these cases, persistence and modeling matter most. Parents can keep offering language without pressure: *"I think you might be feeling nervous—does that sound right?"* Over time, the resistance often softens as children realize the power of self-expression.

The Long-Term Impact

Children with strong emotional vocabulary:

- Regulate emotions more effectively.
- Experience fewer behavioral outbursts.
- Communicate needs clearly in relationships.
- Show greater empathy by recognizing emotions in others.
- Develop resilience by processing rather than suppressing feelings.

By contrast, children without this skill may struggle with anxiety, anger, or relational difficulties, often acting out because they cannot articulate what they feel.

A Parent's Inner Challenge

Teaching emotional vocabulary requires parents to examine their own comfort with emotions. Many adults were raised in homes where feelings were dismissed—*"Stop crying," "Don't be angry."* Parents may find it hard to label or accept emotions in themselves, let alone in their children. Breaking this cycle requires vulnerability: admitting feelings, modeling language, and showing that emotions are human, not shameful.

Parents can ask:

- "Do I label my own emotions out loud?"
- "How do I respond when my child expresses difficult feelings?"
- "Am I teaching my child that emotions are safe to name?"

The answers shape whether children grow up fluent in the language of feelings or silent in the face of them.

Final Takeaway

Emotional vocabulary is more than words—it is power. It is the power to understand oneself, to manage feelings rather than be controlled by them, and to connect with others in meaningful ways. Teaching this skill begins early, grows gradually, and lasts a lifetime. Parents who invest in emotional vocabulary raise children who are not only well-behaved but also emotionally intelligent, resilient, and compassionate. In the end, helping a child find the right words for their feelings is one of the greatest acts of love a parent can offer.

Turning "No" into Teachable Moments

Every parent knows the power and burden of the word *"no."* It may be the most frequently used word in the parenting vocabulary—no running in the street, no more candy, no hitting your sister, no screens before homework. But while "no" is necessary for safety, discipline, and structure, how it is delivered and followed up determines whether it becomes a brick wall or a doorway.

When "no" is used harshly, it can shut down communication, provoke rebellion, or leave children frustrated without understanding why. When "no" is transformed into a teachable moment, however, it becomes an opportunity for growth. It teaches boundaries, self-control, problem-solving, and respect. The goal is not to avoid "no"—it is to use it wisely, turning each instance into a lesson rather than just a rejection.

Why "No" Matters

Children are wired to test limits. "No" provides the essential feedback that boundaries exist. Without it, children may feel entitled, unsafe, or unprepared for the real world. A world without limits would be chaotic and dangerous. Parents who fear saying "no" may create short-term harmony but risk long-term insecurity and poor self-regulation in their children.

Yet, "no" also carries emotional weight. For young children, rejection of a request can feel like rejection of the self. For older children and teens, constant "no's" without explanation may feel controlling, sparking defiance. This is why transforming "no" into a constructive moment is so important.

The Psychology of Resistance

Children often resist "no" not because they are defiant but because they seek autonomy. When they hear "no," they may interpret it as, *"You don't trust me,"* or *"You don't care what I want."*

Developmental psychology shows that autonomy is a core need. If parents say "no" in ways that dismiss children's desires entirely, struggles intensify. If they balance the boundary with empathy and teaching, cooperation grows.

Turning "No" Into "Not This, But That"

One powerful strategy is redirection. Instead of stopping at "no," parents can guide children toward acceptable alternatives:

- Instead of: "No hitting."
- Say: "No hitting. If you're angry, you can use words or stomp your feet."
- Instead of: "No candy before dinner."
- Say: "No candy right now, but you can have some after we eat."

This approach validates desire while reinforcing boundaries, showing that "no" is not rejection but redirection.

Explaining the Why

Children are more likely to accept limits when they understand the reasoning. *"No running in the street"* is more effective when paired with, *"because cars can't always see you, and I want you safe."* The explanation turns a command into a lesson about safety, responsibility, or respect.

Over time, children internalize these lessons, learning not just compliance but wisdom. They begin to anticipate the why themselves, building judgment and self-discipline.

Real-World Example: The Screen Time Battle

Consider a parent whose child asks for more screen time.

Scenario A: The parent says sharply, *"No! Enough already!"* The child protests, argues, or sneaks screens later.

Scenario B: The parent says, *"No more screens right now because your brain needs rest. You can play outside or choose a board game."* The child still feels disappointed but understands the reasoning and sees alternatives. Resistance softens, and the moment becomes a lesson in balance.

The "no" is the same, but the outcome changes because it was used as a teaching tool.

Balancing Empathy With Boundaries

Parents sometimes fear that empathizing with a child's disappointment undermines authority. In fact, empathy strengthens boundaries. Saying, *"I know you're upset we can't go to the park today. It's disappointing when plans change,"* validates the feeling while holding the line. The child learns that emotions are real and acceptable, even when limits remain.

This combination of empathy and firmness models emotional intelligence and builds trust. Children learn: *"My parent hears me, even when I don't get my way."*

The Role of Consistency

For "no" to teach, it must be consistent. If candy is denied before dinner one day but allowed the next, children learn that pushing harder may work. Inconsistency transforms "no" into an invitation for negotiation.

Consistency, on the other hand, turns "no" into a reliable lesson. Over time, children stop pushing as hard, knowing the boundary will hold. This predictability provides security.

Avoiding Power Struggles

When "no" becomes a battleground, both parent and child lose sight of the lesson. Parents can prevent struggles by staying calm, using respectful language, and avoiding escalation. Saying *"I've answered your question, and my decision is final"* communicates authority without hostility.

Sometimes silence is more powerful than repetition. Restating "no" with increasing frustration often fuels conflict. A calm, consistent stance is enough.

Teaching Delayed Gratification

"No" also builds the skill of waiting. Teaching children to accept "not now" instead of immediate gratification prepares them for success in school, work, and relationships. The famous "marshmallow test," where children who delayed eating one marshmallow received two later, showed that self-control predicts long-term achievement. Parents who teach children to wait by using "no" constructively are building this essential skill.

When "No" Should Be Firm and Final

There are moments when "no" cannot be softened—safety issues, disrespectful behavior, or harmful requests. In these cases, explanation still matters, but firmness must be absolute:

- "No, you cannot ride without a seatbelt. It's not safe."
- "No, you may not speak disrespectfully. We use kind words in this family."

Here, "no" teaches not only boundaries but values. The clarity of a firm stance reinforces seriousness.

A Parent's Inner Challenge

Parents often struggle with "no" because of their own histories. Some may have grown up with harsh, unyielding authority and overcompensate by avoiding boundaries. Others may feel guilty disappointing their children and give in too easily. Still others may default to harsh "no's" out of stress, without teaching.

The challenge is to see "no" not as rejection but as guidance. Parents can ask:

- "Do I avoid saying no because I fear conflict?"
- "Do I use no harshly, shutting down communication?"
- "How can I make no both firm and constructive?"

Awareness shifts "no" from reaction to strategy.

Practical Strategies for Parents

1. **Explain When Possible:** Provide reasoning in age-appropriate language.
2. **Offer Alternatives:** Redirect from "no" to acceptable options.
3. **Validate Feelings:** Acknowledge disappointment without reversing the limit.
4. **Stay Calm:** Deliver "no" without anger or sarcasm.
5. **Be Consistent:** Follow through every time to build trust.
6. **Teach Reflection:** After calm is restored, discuss why the limit matters.

The Long-Term Impact

Children raised in environments where "no" is constructive, not punitive, learn to:

- Respect boundaries without fear.
- Delay gratification and practice self-control.
- Accept disappointment while feeling validated.
- Internalize values and reasoning behind rules.
- Communicate respectfully when they face limits in relationships and society.

Children raised where "no" is either absent or harsh may grow entitled or resentful. They may either expect constant accommodation or rebel against authority. Balanced, thoughtful use of "no" creates resilience and respect.

Final Takeaway

"No" is not just a word—it is a teaching moment. Delivered with empathy, clarity, and consistency, it becomes one of the most powerful tools parents have for shaping character. Saying no is not about control; it is about preparation. It equips children to face a world full of boundaries with confidence and wisdom. When parents turn "no" into lessons rather than battles, they give their children a gift: the ability to hear limits, learn from them, and grow stronger.

CHAPTER 5

Discipline That Builds Strength

The Myth of Harsh Punishment

For generations, harsh punishment was considered the backbone of discipline. From spanking to shaming, grounding to yelling, parents believed that making children suffer for their mistakes would make them stronger, more obedient, and more respectful. The logic seemed simple: "If it hurts enough, they won't do it again." Yet decades of research, coupled with the lived experiences of countless families, have revealed a sobering truth—harsh punishment may stop behavior in the short term, but it rarely builds lasting change. In fact, it often creates more harm than good.

Children raised under fear-based discipline may appear obedient, but beneath the surface, they carry wounds: anxiety, resentment, low self-esteem, and weakened trust in authority. They may comply in the moment, but they do not internalize the lessons parents intend. By contrast, children raised with firm but respectful discipline learn responsibility, resilience, and self-control without the scars of shame.

The belief in harsh punishment is one of the most enduring myths of parenting. Dispelling it requires courage: courage to examine traditions, challenge cultural norms, and choose strategies that prioritize long-term growth over short-term control.

Why Harsh Punishment Persists

If research shows harsh punishment is ineffective, why does it continue? Several reasons explain its persistence:

1. **Tradition:** Many parents punish the way they were punished, believing, *"It worked for me, so it must work for my child."*
2. **Immediate Results:** Harsh punishment often produces quick compliance—silencing a tantrum, stopping an argument—which feels like success in the moment.

3. **Stress and Exhaustion:** In moments of frustration, yelling or punitive measures feel easier than calm, intentional responses.
4. **Cultural Beliefs:** Some communities equate strictness with strength, believing permissiveness is the only alternative.
5. **Fear of Losing Control:** Parents may believe that without harsh punishment, children will become unruly or disrespectful.

Understanding these reasons helps parents break the cycle—not with guilt, but with awareness.

What the Research Shows

Decades of studies confirm that harsh punishment does not achieve its intended goals. The American Academy of Pediatrics strongly opposes physical punishment, citing links to increased aggression, antisocial behavior, mental health issues, and damaged parent–child relationships.

Research also shows that children disciplined with harshness are more likely to:

- Obey in the moment but repeat the behavior later.
- Hide mistakes to avoid punishment rather than taking responsibility.
- Develop fear-based compliance rather than self-discipline.
- Experience higher rates of depression, anxiety, and poor self-esteem.

By contrast, children disciplined with consistent, respectful strategies—such as natural consequences, positive reinforcement, and clear boundaries—develop greater responsibility, empathy, and resilience.

The Illusion of Strength

Harsh punishment often gives parents the illusion of strength. A shouted command, a slammed door, or a spanking may silence a child, creating the impression of authority. But silence is not respect—it is fear. Obedience born of fear is fragile. It crumbles when the authority figure is absent, replaced by rebellion or secrecy.

True strength lies not in domination but in guidance. Parents who discipline without harshness still hold firm boundaries, but they do so with calm authority. This kind of strength builds trust, respect, and internal discipline in children.

The Emotional Cost of Harsh Punishment

Children interpret harsh punishment not as, *"I did something wrong,"* but as, *"I am something wrong."* Shame replaces responsibility. Instead of learning to make better choices, children internalize feelings of unworthiness. Over time, this erodes self-esteem, damages the parent–child bond, and creates cycles of anger or withdrawal.

Consider the difference:

- A parent who yells, *"You're so irresponsible!"* teaches shame.
- A parent who calmly says, *"You forgot your homework. Let's think about how to remember next time,"* teaches responsibility.

The first diminishes identity. The second builds skills.

Real-World Example: The Broken Vase

A child knocks over a vase while playing.

Scenario A: The parent yells, spanks the child, and shames them: *"You're always so careless!"* The child cries, fears their parent, and learns to hide future accidents.

Scenario B: The parent stays calm: *"The vase is broken. Let's clean it up together. Next time, play ball outside."* The child learns accountability, problem-solving, and safer choices without fear.

Both situations involve discipline, but only one builds long-term responsibility.

The Cycle of Harshness

Many parents who rely on harsh punishment were raised with it themselves. Without reflection, they repeat what they know. The cycle often sounds like: *"I was spanked, and I turned out fine."* But "fine" often means survival, not thriving. Many adults who say this also struggle with anger, trust issues, or difficulty expressing emotions—legacies of fear-based discipline.

Breaking the cycle means recognizing that surviving harsh punishment does not prove its effectiveness. It proves children are resilient. But resilience should not come at the cost of unnecessary wounds.

Alternatives to Harsh Punishment

Rejecting harsh punishment does not mean abandoning discipline. Children need boundaries, structure, and consequences. The key is using approaches that teach rather than harm:

1. **Natural Consequences:** Letting actions teach. If a child forgets their lunch, they experience hunger and learn to remember next time.
2. **Logical Consequences:** Designed to connect directly to behavior. If toys are not cleaned up, they are unavailable for play.
3. **Positive Reinforcement:** Praising desired behavior increases its frequency.
4. **Time-Ins Instead of Time-Outs:** Sitting with a child during calm-down moments fosters reflection and connection.
5. **Problem-Solving Together:** Inviting children to brainstorm solutions teaches responsibility and collaboration.

These methods maintain authority while building skills, empathy, and resilience.

When Parents Lose Control

Every parent has moments of frustration where harsh words slip out or tempers flare. The goal is not perfection but repair. Apologizing models accountability: *"I yelled earlier because I was frustrated. That wasn't fair. Next time I'll try to stay calm."* Far from weakening authority, this honesty strengthens it. Children learn that mistakes are part of growth—for both parents and children.

Cultural Shifts in Discipline

Society is slowly shifting away from harsh punishment. Schools, pediatric associations, and parenting experts increasingly emphasize positive discipline. Yet many parents fear this shift means permissiveness. The truth is, rejecting harsh punishment is not about removing discipline—it is about improving it. Firm boundaries remain, but they are delivered with respect and guidance rather than fear.

A Parent's Inner Challenge

Moving beyond harsh punishment requires parents to confront their own discomfort with authority. Some worry that without harshness, they will lose control. Others fear being judged by relatives or communities who equate harshness with strength. The real challenge is courage: courage to prioritize long-term growth over appearances, connection over control.

Parents can ask themselves:

- "Do I want my child to obey me out of fear or respect?"
- "What lesson will my child carry from this moment—shame or responsibility?"
- "Am I repeating patterns from my childhood, or choosing intentionally?"

These reflections help shift discipline from reaction to strategy.

The Long-Term Impact

Children raised without harsh punishment—but with firm, respectful discipline—develop:

- Stronger self-esteem, because mistakes are corrected without shame.
- Greater trust in parents, because authority is paired with respect.
- Better emotional regulation, because they learn calm responses rather than fear.
- Higher responsibility, because consequences teach rather than punish.
- Healthier relationships, because they model respect in their own interactions.

By contrast, children raised with harsh punishment may appear obedient but often struggle with fear, resentment, or rebellion later.

Final Takeaway

The myth of harsh punishment is rooted in the illusion of strength and the seduction of quick results. But true discipline is not about control—it is about teaching. Harsh punishment silences behavior without shaping character. Respectful, firm guidance builds responsibility, resilience, and trust. The most powerful parents are not those who make their children fear them, but those who teach their children to respect themselves, others, and the world. Dispelling the myth of harsh punishment frees families from cycles of fear and opens the path to growth.

Natural and Logical Consequences That Work

Every parent faces the challenge of teaching discipline: how to help children understand that their choices have results. For many, the instinct is to impose punishments—grounding, yelling, or taking away privileges—often unrelated to the behavior itself. While these methods may stop misbehavior in the moment, they rarely teach the lesson intended. Children comply out of fear or resentment rather than understanding.

Natural and logical consequences offer a more effective, respectful, and lasting alternative. Instead of punishing children for mistakes, they allow children to experience the real-world results of their actions or carefully designed consequences that make sense. These methods teach responsibility, accountability, and problem-solving in ways punishment never can.

Why Consequences Matter

Children are not born knowing how the world works. They must learn that actions have effects—both positive and negative. Consequences are how this lesson is taught. Without them, children grow entitled, expecting rules to bend. With harsh or arbitrary consequences, children grow resentful, feeling controlled rather than guided.

Natural and logical consequences strike the balance: they connect choices to outcomes, allowing children to learn through experience. The message becomes: *"Your decisions matter. You are capable of learning from them."*

The Difference Between Punishment and Consequences

Punishment is about making children suffer for misbehavior. It is often unrelated to the offense: a child forgets homework, so they lose dessert. A teenager talks back, so they are grounded from seeing friends. While these tactics may satisfy a parent's frustration, they do not teach cause and effect.

Consequences, by contrast, are either natural (arising from reality) or logical (created by parents but directly connected to the behavior). For example:

- **Natural:** A child refuses to wear a coat; they feel cold.
- **Logical:** A child refuses to put away toys; the toys are put away by the parent and unavailable for the next day.

Both approaches connect action to outcome, teaching responsibility without shaming.

The Power of Natural Consequences

Natural consequences are the most powerful teachers because they are real-life experiences. No lecture is needed; the world provides the lesson. A child who leaves their bike in the rain discovers it rusts. A teenager who procrastinates learns the stress of rushing homework.

Parents sometimes try to shield children from all discomfort, but this robs them of learning. Experiencing small failures in childhood prepares children for bigger challenges later. Natural consequences work best when:

- Safety is not at risk.
- The consequence is immediate and clear.
- Parents remain supportive rather than punitive.

For example, when a child forgets lunch, a parent may resist rescuing them. Instead, allowing hunger to teach responsibility sends a stronger message than any lecture could.

The Role of Logical Consequences

Not all behaviors allow for natural consequences, especially when safety, respect, or fairness is at stake. This is where logical consequences are essential. These are consequences intentionally designed by parents to connect to behavior in meaningful ways.

For example:

- If a child colors on the wall, they help clean it.
- If siblings fight over a toy, the toy is removed until they agree to share.
- If a teen misses curfew, their freedom is reduced until trust is rebuilt.

Logical consequences are effective when they are:

1. **Related:** Directly connected to the behavior.
2. **Respectful:** Delivered without shaming or hostility.
3. **Reasonable:** Proportionate to the offense.
4. **Revealed in Advance:** Children understand the rules and results beforehand.

These qualities ensure that consequences teach rather than punish.

Real-World Example: The Messy Bedroom

Scenario A: A parent sees a messy bedroom and yells: *"You're grounded until it's clean!"* The child complies angrily, resenting the punishment and learning little.

Scenario B: The parent calmly says: *"The room must be clean before friends come over. If it's not, the visit will be postponed."* The consequence is logical—messy room, no visitors. The child learns responsibility without hostility.

The second approach fosters growth; the first fosters resentment.

Why Consequences Work Better Than Punishment

1. **They Teach Cause and Effect:** Children see the connection between choices and outcomes.
2. **They Build Internal Motivation:** Instead of avoiding punishment, children learn to make better choices for their own sake.
3. **They Preserve Relationships:** Respectful consequences maintain trust and connection between parent and child.
4. **They Encourage Problem-Solving:** Children learn not just what *not* to do, but what to do differently next time.

The Role of Empathy in Consequences

Some parents fear that consequences must be delivered harshly to be effective. In reality, empathy strengthens their impact. Saying, *"I know it's disappointing you can't use your toy today because it wasn't put away. Tomorrow you can try again,"* validates feelings while holding firm. The child feels understood, even in disappointment, making the lesson more likely to stick.

Avoiding Common Pitfalls

- **Overdoing It:** Consequences that are extreme lose credibility. For example, banning screens for a month because of one late homework assignment teaches resentment, not responsibility.
- **Inconsistency:** If consequences are enforced sometimes but not others, children learn to gamble.
- **Unclear Rules:** Consequences must be tied to clear expectations. Vague rules create confusion.
- **Rescuing Too Soon:** Parents often step in to soften natural consequences. Allowing small failures builds resilience.

Cultural Perspectives on Consequences

In some cultures, discipline traditionally leans toward harsh punishment, while others emphasize negotiation or collective responsibility. Natural and logical consequences provide a middle ground that respects cultural values while ensuring children learn accountability. They offer structure without harshness, guidance without permissiveness.

A Parent's Inner Challenge

Implementing consequences requires patience and self-control. Parents under stress may default to yelling or punitive punishments. It takes discipline to pause, think, and choose a consequence that teaches rather than harms. Parents can ask themselves:

- "Does this consequence teach the lesson I want?"
- "Is it connected to the behavior or just my frustration?"
- "Am I using this moment to guide, or to control?"

By shifting mindset, parents move from reaction to intentional teaching.

Long-Term Benefits of Natural and Logical Consequences

Children raised with consistent, respectful consequences develop:

- **Responsibility:** They understand actions have results.
- **Resilience:** They learn to recover from mistakes.
- **Self-Control:** They internalize limits rather than relying on external threats.
- **Respect for Authority:** They see rules as fair, not arbitrary.
- **Problem-Solving Skills:** They practice finding solutions to avoid repeated mistakes.

In contrast, children raised with punishment often learn to hide mistakes, fear authority, or rebel once external control is removed.

Final Takeaway

Natural and logical consequences are not about letting children suffer, nor about controlling them harshly. They are about teaching. They say: *"Your choices matter. You are capable of learning from them."* Unlike punishment, which silences behavior without teaching, consequences connect action to outcome, fostering responsibility, resilience, and respect. When parents replace arbitrary punishments with thoughtful consequences, they transform discipline from fear into growth—and raise children prepared for the real world.

Using Time-Ins Instead of Time-Outs

For decades, the "time-out" has been one of the most popular parenting tools. The idea is simple: when a child misbehaves, they are removed from the situation, placed alone in a chair or corner, and told to think about what they did. On the surface, it seems logical— time-outs stop behavior and give parents a moment of peace. Yet while time-outs may calm the parent's frustration, they often do little to teach the child. Worse, they can leave children feeling isolated, shamed, or misunderstood.

An alternative has emerged from developmental psychology: the "time-in." Unlike time-outs, time-ins focus not on exclusion but on connection. Instead of sending children away, parents sit with them, help them calm down, and guide them toward understanding and repair. This simple shift transforms discipline from punishment to teaching. It replaces shame with empathy, isolation with relationship, and fear with learning.

Why Time-Outs Fall Short

Time-outs are meant to give children space to calm down. But for many children, especially younger ones, isolation escalates distress rather than soothing it. A child sent to a corner often feels abandoned, rejected, or angry—not reflective. Instead of thinking about their behavior, they may think: *"My parent doesn't love me when I'm bad."*

Other problems with time-outs include:

- **They don't teach alternatives.** Children learn what not to do, but not what to do instead.
- **They can damage trust.** Repeated isolation may make children less likely to open up when struggling.
- **They can trigger power struggles.** Children resist, refuse to sit still, or escalate behavior, undermining the purpose.
- **They shift focus from behavior to punishment.** The lesson becomes about enduring isolation, not making better choices.

Time-outs may stop behavior temporarily, but they rarely build long-term self-regulation.

The Concept of Time-Ins

A time-in flips the script. Instead of sending children away, parents stay present. The child is invited to sit with the parent, calm their body, and talk through what happened once emotions settle. The message is: *"Even when you make mistakes, you are not alone. I will help you learn to manage your feelings and choices."*

Time-ins don't mean ignoring misbehavior. They hold boundaries firmly. But they do so with empathy, ensuring that discipline strengthens rather than weakens connection.

The Science of Connection

Attachment theory emphasizes that children regulate emotions best in the presence of a secure caregiver. Left alone, especially during distress, many children cannot self-soothe. Their developing brains need co-regulation—an adult's calm presence to help them return to balance. Time-ins provide this co-regulation, allowing children to calm down faster and learn more effectively.

Neuroscience supports this approach. When children are dysregulated, their prefrontal cortex (responsible for reasoning) goes offline. Isolation does not restore it; connection does. Sitting with a calm, supportive adult helps re-engage the thinking brain, making reflection possible.

Real-World Example: The Playground Incident

Imagine a child pushes another at the playground.

Scenario A: The parent yells, sends the child to a bench for five minutes, and ignores them. The child sulks, feeling angry and ashamed. They return no wiser, likely to repeat the behavior.

Scenario B: The parent takes the child aside, sits together, and says calmly: *"You were angry and pushed. That hurt your friend. Let's take some deep breaths, then talk about what else you could have done."* The child feels guided, not abandoned. They learn both accountability and alternatives.

The difference is profound. One isolates; the other teaches.

How to Use Time-Ins Effectively

1. **Stay Calm Yourself:** Parents must regulate before guiding. If emotions are high, take a moment to breathe before engaging.
2. **Invite, Don't Force:** Encourage the child to sit nearby rather than dragging them. Resistance decreases when connection feels safe.
3. **Co-Regulate First:** Begin with calming strategies—deep breaths, hugs if welcomed, or quiet presence—before discussing behavior.
4. **Name the Feelings:** Help the child put words to emotions: *"You were frustrated when the block tower fell."*
5. **Teach Alternatives:** Guide the child toward healthier responses: *"Next time, you can ask for help instead of yelling."*
6. **Repair and Reconnect:** If others were harmed, encourage apologies or amends. End with reassurance of love: *"I know you can do better, and I love you even when you make mistakes."*

Time-Ins by Age

Toddlers: Focus on calming and simple language. Sit with them, label feelings, and redirect gently.

Elementary-Age Children: Add reflection. After calming, discuss what happened and brainstorm alternatives.

Adolescents: Allow space, but remain available. A teen may not want close proximity, but a calm presence and open conversation afterward still embody the spirit of time-ins.

Addressing Misconceptions About Time-Ins

Some parents worry that time-ins are "soft" or permissive. In reality, they are firm and demanding: they require parents to stay engaged, guide reflection, and enforce accountability. Time-ins do not remove consequences; they make them constructive. For example, after a time-in, a child who broke a rule may still lose a privilege—but they also understand why.

Avoiding Pitfalls

- **Don't Lecture Mid-Crisis:** Children can't absorb lessons until they're calm. Wait until emotions settle.
- **Don't Rescue From Responsibility:** Connection does not erase consequences. A time-in should end with accountability, not avoidance.
- **Don't Overuse:** Time-ins are for significant misbehavior or emotional overwhelm, not every small disagreement.

A Parent's Inner Challenge

Time-ins require patience, and many parents find them harder than time-outs. Sitting with a child in distress is emotionally taxing. Parents raised with harsh punishment may feel uncomfortable offering comfort during misbehavior. Others may worry about judgment from peers or relatives. Overcoming these challenges means redefining strength: true strength is not in punishing but in teaching with presence.

Parents can reflect:

- "Am I avoiding connection because it feels uncomfortable for me?"
- "Do I mistake harshness for authority?"
- "What long-term lessons do I want my child to carry from discipline?"

These questions guide parents toward intentional, effective strategies.

The Long-Term Impact of Time-Ins

Children raised with time-ins learn:

- **Emotional Regulation:** They practice calming with support, eventually internalizing the skill.
- **Accountability:** They connect actions to impact without shame.
- **Trust:** They see discipline as guidance, not rejection.
- **Empathy:** They experience respect even in correction, making them more likely to extend respect to others.

In contrast, children raised primarily with time-outs may learn compliance but also internalize rejection, fear, or resentment.

Final Takeaway

Time-outs remove children from misbehavior but often fail to teach. Time-ins transform discipline into a moment of connection, reflection, and growth. They hold firm boundaries while preserving dignity, teaching children that mistakes are not grounds for rejection but opportunities for learning. In choosing time-ins, parents move from punishment to partnership, raising children who are not only better behaved in the moment but also more resilient, responsible, and emotionally intelligent in the long run.

Reward Systems That Encourage Resilience

Rewards are a powerful tool in parenting. When used wisely, they motivate children, reinforce positive behavior, and make family life smoother. Yet many parents worry: *"Am I bribing my child?"* or *"Will rewards make them dependent on external praise instead of developing inner drive?"* These are valid concerns. Rewards can backfire if they are misused, fostering entitlement or short-term compliance without building character.

But when reward systems are designed with purpose, they do more than shape behavior—they cultivate resilience, self-discipline, and confidence. The key is not in the presence of rewards but in how they are structured, presented, and gradually shifted toward intrinsic motivation.

Why Rewards Work

Rewards tap into the brain's natural learning systems. When a child receives a positive outcome for a behavior, dopamine is released, strengthening the neural pathway for that action. Over time, the child associates effort with success, motivation, and satisfaction. This process, studied extensively in behavioral psychology, explains why reinforcement works across species and settings—from classrooms to workplaces.

For children, rewards are concrete signals: *"This behavior matters. Keep doing it."* Used well, they encourage effort, persistence, and responsibility.

Rewards vs. Bribes

Parents often confuse rewards with bribes. The difference lies in timing and intention.

- **Bribe:** Offered during misbehavior to stop it. Example: *"If you stop crying in the store, I'll buy you candy."* This reinforces the tantrum itself.
- **Reward:** Planned in advance, connected to desired behavior. Example: *"When we finish shopping without tantrums, you can choose a healthy snack."* This reinforces cooperation, not misbehavior.

Rewards motivate; bribes manipulate. The key distinction is whether the system is proactive (teaching) or reactive (appeasing).

The Problem with Material Rewards

Material rewards—stickers, toys, money—can be useful tools, especially for young children. But overreliance on them creates risks:

- Children may focus only on external gain.
- Rewards may need to escalate to maintain motivation.
- Intrinsic motivation ("I do this because it's right") may weaken.

This does not mean material rewards should never be used, but they should be paired with intrinsic reinforcements—praise, pride, competence—and gradually phased out as children internalize habits.

Designing Effective Reward Systems

Reward systems succeed when they are structured around clear expectations, fairness, and gradual progression. Key principles include:

1. **Clarity:** Children know exactly which behavior earns rewards.
2. **Consistency:** Rewards are given predictably, not sporadically.
3. **Proportion:** Rewards match effort—not so lavish they spoil, not so trivial they lose meaning.
4. **Progression:** Systems evolve with age and maturity, shifting from external rewards to internal satisfaction.

Real-World Example: Homework Motivation

A child struggles to complete homework.

Scenario A: The parent scolds, threatens punishment, and demands compliance. The child resists, completing work reluctantly or dishonestly.

Scenario B: The parent creates a system: each day homework is completed without argument, the child earns a token. Five tokens can be exchanged for extra playtime or a family activity. Alongside tokens, the parent offers praise: *"I'm proud of how you focused today."*

Over time, the child begins to associate homework not only with rewards but also with personal competence. The system transitions from external motivation to internal pride.

Types of Reward Systems

1. Token Systems: Children earn points, stickers, or tokens for positive behaviors. Tokens can be traded for privileges (choosing dinner, extra bedtime story, family outing). Effective for younger children.

2. Privilege Rewards: Instead of material goods, rewards involve experiences—extra playtime, picking a movie, hosting a friend. Builds appreciation for non-material joys.

3. Social Rewards: Praise, recognition, and attention are often the most powerful reinforcers. *"You worked hard on that puzzle—I'm impressed with your persistence."*

4. Family-Based Rewards: Collective goals (like a family game night earned by everyone completing chores) foster teamwork and shared responsibility.

Encouraging Resilience Through Rewards

The true goal of reward systems is not obedience but resilience—the ability to cope with setbacks, persist through challenges, and recover from failure. Rewards can encourage resilience when they focus on effort, persistence, and problem-solving rather than perfection.

Examples:

- Rewarding a child for trying again after a mistake.
- Recognizing persistence on a difficult task, even if the outcome isn't perfect.
- Celebrating progress toward a goal, not just final success.

This approach teaches children that growth matters more than instant results. They learn to value effort, adapt to obstacles, and keep trying.

Avoiding Common Pitfalls

1. **Rewarding Only Outcomes:** If rewards are tied only to success (like perfect grades), children may fear failure. Instead, reward effort, strategy, and persistence.
2. **Inconsistency:** Sporadic rewards confuse children. Consistency builds trust in the system.
3. **Overuse:** Constant rewards dilute meaning. Use them strategically for new habits or challenging behaviors.
4. **Withholding Affection:** Love should never be conditional on rewards. Affection must remain constant.

Building Intrinsic Motivation

The ultimate goal is for children to move from doing the right thing for external rewards to doing it because it feels right. Parents can facilitate this by:

- Pairing rewards with verbal recognition of effort and values.

- Asking reflective questions: *"How did it feel to finish your homework before dinner?"*
- Gradually phasing out tangible rewards as habits form.

Over time, children internalize satisfaction, moving from *"I do this for a sticker"* to *"I do this because it makes me proud."*

A Parent's Inner Challenge

Some parents worry that rewards spoil children, while others lean on them too heavily. Finding balance requires reflection:

- "Am I rewarding effort, or only perfection?"
- "Am I teaching my child to seek approval, or to build pride in themselves?"
- "Am I using rewards as tools for growth, or as shortcuts for compliance?"

When parents see rewards as scaffolding—temporary supports until intrinsic motivation develops—they use them wisely.

Long-Term Benefits of Thoughtful Reward Systems

Children raised with effective reward systems learn to:

- Value effort and persistence.
- Build self-confidence from achievements.
- Develop intrinsic motivation as rewards fade.
- Approach challenges with resilience.
- Appreciate non-material joys like praise, connection, and shared experiences.

By contrast, children raised with inconsistent, manipulative, or purely material rewards may learn to comply only for gain, struggle with entitlement, or fear failure.

Final Takeaway

Reward systems are neither magic nor manipulative—they are tools. When used thoughtfully, they encourage effort, persistence, and responsibility while building resilience. They shift from external motivation to internal pride, teaching children that discipline is not about avoiding punishment but about embracing growth. Parents who design reward systems with care raise children who are not only cooperative in the moment but also motivated, confident, and resilient for life.

Teaching Responsibility Through Accountability

One of the greatest goals of parenting is to raise children who take responsibility for their actions—not out of fear, but out of integrity. Responsibility is the foundation of independence, resilience, and trust. Yet responsibility cannot be forced; it must be taught, practiced, and reinforced through accountability.

Accountability is not about blame or shame. It is about helping children connect choices to outcomes, repair mistakes, and recognize their role in relationships and community. When accountability is modeled and nurtured, children grow into adults who own their decisions, contribute positively to society, and face challenges with maturity. Without accountability, children may avoid responsibility, shift blame, or expect others to clean up their messes.

Teaching responsibility through accountability is not just about correcting misbehavior—it is about building character.

Why Responsibility Matters

Children who develop responsibility learn essential life skills:

- **Self-Discipline:** Managing time, completing tasks, and meeting commitments.
- **Integrity:** Doing the right thing even when no one is watching.
- **Resilience:** Recovering from mistakes by owning them and trying again.
- **Trustworthiness:** Being reliable in relationships at home, school, and eventually the workplace.

Without responsibility, children may grow into adults who struggle with independence, rely on others to solve problems, or avoid challenges.

The Role of Accountability

Accountability is the process that teaches responsibility. It means helping children:

1. Recognize their actions and choices.
2. Accept the consequences of those actions.
3. Repair harm when possible.
4. Learn strategies for improvement.

Accountability is not about making children feel bad—it is about making them feel capable of doing better.

Accountability vs. Blame

Parents sometimes confuse accountability with blame. Blame shames the child: *"You're so careless!"* Accountability addresses behavior: *"You forgot your homework; what can you do to remember tomorrow?"*

The difference is profound:

- **Blame** erodes self-esteem and teaches avoidance.
- **Accountability** builds resilience and teaches responsibility.

Real-World Example: The Forgotten Chores

Scenario A: A child forgets to take out the trash. The parent yells: *"You're so irresponsible!"* The child feels shamed, angry, and less motivated to try.

Scenario B: The parent says: *"The trash wasn't taken out, so now the kitchen smells. What can you do differently tomorrow to make sure it gets done?"* The child reflects, accepts responsibility, and learns strategies (like setting a reminder). Accountability builds competence instead of resentment.

Practical Ways to Teach Accountability

1. **Model It Yourself:** Parents who admit mistakes show children what accountability looks like. *"I was short-tempered earlier. I'm sorry. Next time, I'll take a breath first."*
2. **Focus on Behavior, Not Character:** Correct the action, not the child's worth.
3. **Require Repair:** If a child hurts a sibling, accountability means apologizing or making amends—not just saying sorry, but repairing trust.
4. **Encourage Problem-Solving:** Ask questions like: *"What could you do differently next time?"* instead of prescribing answers.
5. **Hold Consistent Consequences:** Let children experience the outcomes of their actions, whether natural or logical.
6. **Celebrate Ownership:** Praise when children admit mistakes. *"I appreciate that you told the truth about what happened."*

Age-Appropriate Accountability

Toddlers: Focus on simple cause and effect. If they spill, they help wipe it up. Accountability is framed as learning, not blame.

Elementary-Age Children: Introduce responsibility for chores, homework, and friendships. Guide them to reflect on their role in problems and solutions.

Adolescents: Increase responsibility for time management, commitments, and relationships. Encourage accountability through open conversations, natural consequences, and involvement in family decision-making.

Accountability in School and Community

Responsibility extends beyond the home. Parents can reinforce accountability by connecting children's actions to the broader community:

- If a child disrupts class, accountability may include apologizing to the teacher and classmates.
- If a teen breaks a rule in sports, accountability means addressing the team.

These experiences teach that responsibility is not just personal—it is relational.

Avoiding Common Pitfalls

- **Over-Rescuing:** Parents who swoop in to fix every mistake rob children of accountability. Forgetting homework once is a powerful teacher; parents who deliver it each time prevent learning.
- **Excessive Harshness:** Overly punitive responses create fear, not responsibility. Children may learn to hide mistakes rather than own them.

- **Inconsistency:** When accountability is enforced sometimes but ignored other times, children learn to gamble with responsibility.

Accountability Builds Resilience

Owning mistakes without shame builds resilience. Children learn that failure is not final—it is feedback. They see that repairing harm and trying again is part of growth. Instead of avoiding risks, they embrace challenges, knowing they can recover from setbacks.

This resilience is one of the greatest gifts accountability provides. A child who learns, *"I can make mistakes, fix them, and move forward,"* becomes an adult who thrives in the face of adversity.

A Parent's Inner Challenge

Many parents struggle with teaching accountability because of their own experiences. Some were raised with harsh blame, leaving them fearful of repeating that cycle. Others were overprotected, never learning accountability themselves.

The challenge is balance: holding children accountable without shaming, supporting them without rescuing. Parents can reflect:

- "Do I step in too quickly to fix my child's mistakes?"
- "Do I use shame instead of guidance?"
- "Do I model accountability in my own life?"

Awareness turns accountability from reaction into intention.

Long-Term Impact of Accountability

Children raised with accountability learn to:

- Own their choices without excuses.
- Repair relationships when harm is done.

- Approach challenges with maturity.
- Develop independence and reliability.
- Build stronger self-esteem by seeing themselves as capable of change.

In contrast, children without accountability may grow into adults who avoid responsibility, blame others, or collapse under challenges.

Final Takeaway

Teaching responsibility through accountability is one of the most powerful ways to prepare children for adulthood. Accountability is not blame—it is empowerment. It teaches children that their choices matter, that mistakes can be repaired, and that resilience grows from owning challenges. Parents who model and nurture accountability raise children who are not only responsible at home but also trustworthy, resilient, and prepared for life.

CHAPTER 6

Building Emotional Resilience

Helping Kids Cope with Frustration

Frustration is an inevitable part of childhood. Toys break, games are lost, homework feels impossible, siblings take turns too slowly, and bedtime always seems to arrive too soon. For children, whose brains are still developing self-regulation skills, frustration can feel overwhelming. Their instinctive responses are often explosive—crying, yelling, slamming doors, or giving up entirely.

Parents often find these reactions exhausting, yet frustration is not the enemy. It is an essential teacher. Learning to cope with frustration builds resilience, perseverance, and problem-solving—the very qualities children need to thrive in school, relationships, and life. The challenge is not to eliminate frustration from children's lives but to equip them with the tools to face it constructively.

Why Frustration Matters

Frustration is the gap between desire and reality. It arises when children want something they cannot have, expect success but face difficulty, or feel powerless in a situation. While uncomfortable, frustration plays a critical developmental role:

- **It fuels growth.** Struggling through frustration teaches persistence.
- **It strengthens problem-solving.** Children learn to adapt when things don't go as planned.
- **It builds resilience.** Facing frustration without giving up prepares children for bigger challenges later in life.

Without opportunities to face frustration, children risk becoming easily discouraged, entitled, or avoidant of challenges.

The Science of Frustration

Neuroscience shows that frustration activates the amygdala—the brain's emotional alarm center. This triggers fight, flight, or freeze responses: tantrums, withdrawal, or stubborn refusal. Children's prefrontal cortex, which regulates emotions and supports rational thinking, is still developing well into adolescence. This explains why children often react impulsively when frustrated.

The good news is that repeated practice with frustration builds neural connections for self-regulation. Each time a child calms down, problem-solves, or persists through difficulty, their brain strengthens pathways for resilience. Parents are key coaches in this process.

Common Triggers of Frustration

- **Tasks That Feel Too Hard:** Homework, puzzles, or sports challenges.
- **Unmet Desires:** Wanting a toy, snack, or privilege denied.
- **Loss of Control:** Siblings changing rules, parents setting boundaries.
- **Transitions:** Moving from fun to chores, or from home to school.
- **Perfectionism:** Expecting immediate success and collapsing at mistakes.

Recognizing these triggers allows parents to anticipate and guide children through them.

The Parent's Role

Parents cannot—and should not—remove frustration entirely. Instead, their role is to support children in facing it. This means:

1. **Modeling Calm:** Children mirror adult responses. If parents panic, yell, or give up easily, children copy. If parents stay calm and persistent, children learn by example.

2. **Providing Tools:** Teaching coping strategies children can use independently.
3. **Balancing Support and Independence:** Offering help without rescuing, so children build competence.

Real-World Example: The Puzzle Meltdown

A five-year-old struggles to fit puzzle pieces together.

Scenario A: The parent says, *"Stop crying, I'll do it for you."* The puzzle is completed, but the child learns helplessness.

Scenario B: The parent says, *"I see you're frustrated. Take a deep breath. Try turning the piece another way. You can do this."* The child persists, solves the puzzle, and beams with pride.

In the second scenario, frustration became fuel for learning.

Teaching Coping Strategies

Children need practical tools to manage frustration. Parents can introduce and practice these skills regularly:

1. **Deep Breathing:** Simple techniques like "smell the flower, blow the candle" calm the nervous system.
2. **Positive Self-Talk:** Teach phrases like, *"I can try again,"* or *"Mistakes help me learn."*
3. **Break Down Tasks:** Encourage tackling challenges step by step instead of all at once.
4. **Take Breaks:** Short pauses prevent overwhelm without giving up.
5. **Use Humor:** Laughing together lightens frustration and resets perspective.
6. **Problem-Solving Together:** Ask, *"What else could we try?"* to shift focus from failure to solutions.

Encouraging Persistence

Praise plays a crucial role in helping children cope with frustration. But praise must focus on effort, not just outcome. Saying, *"You worked so hard on that problem,"* is more powerful than, *"You're so smart."* Effort-based praise encourages persistence even when success is not immediate.

Parents can also model persistence in their own lives: cooking a difficult recipe, fixing something broken, or learning a new skill while narrating the process of trial and error. Children absorb the message: effort is valuable, mistakes are normal, and frustration is temporary.

When to Step In and When to Step Back

Parents often wrestle with the question: *"Should I help or let my child struggle?"* The answer depends on balance. Too much help fosters dependence; too little creates despair. The goal is to step in as a coach, not a rescuer:

- Offer encouragement and hints.
- Break down the challenge into smaller steps.
- Remain nearby as emotional support.

Over time, gradually step back to allow independence as confidence grows.

Frustration and Emotional Vocabulary

Children who lack words for their feelings often express frustration through behavior—tantrums, yelling, or sulking. Teaching emotional vocabulary helps them identify and express frustration constructively. A parent might say: *"You seem frustrated because the tower keeps falling. That makes sense."* Labeling the emotion reduces its intensity and opens the door to coping strategies.

The Risk of Shielding Children from Frustration

Many well-meaning parents overprotect children from discomfort, rushing to fix problems before they arise. While this prevents tears in the short term, it robs children of resilience. A child who never experiences small frustrations may collapse at larger challenges later.

Allowing children to struggle within safe limits builds frustration tolerance. Small frustrations in childhood—like losing a game or redoing homework—prepare them for life's bigger setbacks.

Real-World Example: The Soccer Game

A child loses a soccer game and bursts into tears: *"It's not fair!"*

Scenario A: The parent dismisses: *"Stop crying, it's just a game."* The child feels invalidated and avoids future challenges.

Scenario B: The parent validates: *"I know losing feels really hard. You played with effort, and I'm proud of you. What can we practice for next time?"* The child learns to process frustration, recover, and grow.

The second response transforms loss into resilience.

Cultural Views of Frustration

Cultures vary in how frustration is approached. Some emphasize toughness—children are expected to endure silently. Others encourage expression—children are taught to voice feelings openly. Both approaches have strengths and risks. The most effective path combines validation of emotions with encouragement of resilience: *"It's okay to feel frustrated. And you are strong enough to handle it."*

A Parent's Inner Challenge

Parents' own relationship with frustration often shapes their responses. Adults who grew up with harsh punishment may see frustration as weakness. Others, raised with overprotection, may feel compelled to rescue children from every challenge. Recognizing these patterns allows parents to choose intentionally.

Questions to reflect on:

- "How do I handle my own frustration?"
- "Do I model persistence or giving up?"
- "Do I rush to fix problems, or allow space for struggle?"

Awareness helps parents guide children more effectively.

Long-Term Benefits of Coping With Frustration

Children who learn to cope with frustration develop:

- **Resilience:** They recover quickly from setbacks.
- **Problem-Solving Skills:** They find creative solutions under pressure.
- **Confidence:** They see themselves as capable of overcoming obstacles.
- **Emotional Intelligence:** They identify, express, and regulate feelings.
- **Perseverance:** They persist in school, hobbies, and relationships.

In contrast, children shielded from frustration—or punished harshly for expressing it—may grow into adults who fear challenges, give up easily, or lash out at obstacles.

Final Takeaway

Frustration is not a sign of failure but an invitation to grow. Children who learn to cope with it gain resilience, persistence, and confidence. Parents play a vital role—not by removing frustration, but by guiding children through it with empathy, tools, and encouragement. When handled well, frustration transforms from a source of tantrums into a teacher of strength. In helping children cope with frustration, parents prepare them not just for childhood challenges but for the inevitable struggles of life, equipping them to face the world with courage and resilience.

Teaching Problem-Solving Skills Early

When a toy breaks, when siblings fight, when homework feels impossible, or when a playground disagreement erupts, children are faced with problems both big and small. For many, the instinctive reaction is to cry, lash out, or give up. But what if children could instead pause, think through options, and choose constructive solutions? This is the power of problem-solving.

Problem-solving is not only an academic or intellectual skill; it is a life skill. Children who learn to solve problems early grow into adults who approach challenges with creativity, resilience, and confidence. Without this skill, they may avoid responsibility, collapse in the face of obstacles, or depend excessively on others to rescue them.

Teaching problem-solving early gives children a foundation for independence. It transforms conflict and mistakes into opportunities for growth.

Why Problem-Solving Matters

Everyday life is filled with challenges. Children must learn to navigate these challenges not just by obeying rules but by thinking critically. Problem-solving teaches them to:

- **Take Responsibility:** Recognize that their choices affect outcomes.
- **Think Creatively:** Explore multiple possibilities instead of reacting impulsively.
- **Develop Resilience:** Persist in the face of setbacks.
- **Build Independence:** Trust themselves to make decisions.
- **Strengthen Relationships:** Resolve conflicts respectfully instead of escalating them.

Problem-solving is the bridge between frustration and resilience.

The Brain and Problem-Solving

Neuroscience shows that problem-solving engages the prefrontal cortex—the area responsible for planning, reasoning, and decision-making. This part of the brain develops gradually throughout childhood and adolescence. The more children practice problem-solving, the stronger these neural pathways become. In other words, solving problems is like exercising a muscle—the earlier and more often it is used, the stronger it grows.

Real-World Example: The Playground Dispute

Two children argue over a swing.

Scenario A: The parent intervenes, decides who gets the swing, and ends the conflict. The problem is solved externally, but the children learn dependence, not resolution.

Scenario B: The parent coaches the children: *"You both want the swing. What are some ways you could solve this together?"* They suggest taking turns or setting a timer. The children practice negotiation, compromise, and creativity.

The second approach builds lifelong skills.

Steps for Teaching Problem-Solving

Children are not born knowing how to solve problems; they must be taught. A simple framework helps:

1. **Identify the Problem:** Teach children to state the issue clearly. *"We both want the same toy."*
2. **Brainstorm Solutions:** Encourage multiple ideas, no matter how silly. This builds creativity.
3. **Evaluate Options:** Discuss which ideas are fair, safe, and respectful.
4. **Choose a Plan:** Pick one solution together.
5. **Try It Out:** Put the plan into action.
6. **Reflect:** Did it work? If not, adjust and try again.

This process can be modeled repeatedly until children internalize it.

Problem-Solving Through Play

Play is a natural training ground for problem-solving. Building blocks that collapse, board games that require strategy, or pretend play scenarios all create opportunities for children to practice. Parents can encourage reflection by asking: *"What could you do differently next time?"* or *"How else could we build this tower?"*

Games that require teamwork, like puzzles or cooperative board games, also teach negotiation, patience, and compromise.

The Role of Questions

Asking guiding questions is one of the most powerful tools for teaching problem-solving. Instead of giving answers, parents can prompt thinking:

- "What do you think will happen if you try that?"
- "How else could you solve this?"
- "What would make this fair for everyone?"

- "What could you do differently next time?"

Questions shift responsibility from the parent to the child, building independence.

Teaching Emotional Regulation Alongside Problem-Solving

Children cannot solve problems when overwhelmed by emotion. Teaching calming strategies—deep breathing, naming feelings, taking short breaks—prepares them to think clearly. Once calm, they are better able to move into problem-solving mode.

Parents can model this by narrating their own process: *"I was frustrated when the sink broke, so I took a breath, then made a plan to fix it."* Children see that emotions and problem-solving can coexist.

Real-World Example: The Homework Struggle

A child refuses to start homework, saying, *"It's too hard!"*

Scenario A: The parent demands compliance: *"Just do it now!"* The child cries and resists further.

Scenario B: The parent says: *"I hear that it feels hard. Let's think of a way to make it easier. Should we start with the first problem together, or take a five-minute break and then try?"* The child learns to break challenges into manageable steps.

The second approach fosters problem-solving rather than avoidance.

Building Problem-Solving into Daily Life

Parents can weave problem-solving into everyday routines:

- **Meals:** If a child dislikes dinner, ask, *"What could you add to make it better?"*
- **Chores:** If a child forgets chores, ask, *"What system could help you remember?"*
- **Schedules:** If activities conflict, ask, *"How could we make this work fairly?"*

Each small moment becomes practice.

Encouraging Persistence

Problem-solving is not always immediate. Children must learn to persist when the first solution fails. Parents can encourage persistence by normalizing trial and error: *"That didn't work, but let's try another way."* Over time, children see failure not as defeat but as feedback.

Avoiding Common Pitfalls

- **Solving Problems for Children:** This robs them of learning. Coaching is better than rescuing.
- **Over-Criticizing Ideas:** Dismissing children's suggestions too quickly discourages creativity. Encourage all ideas before evaluating.
- **Focusing Only on Outcomes:** Praise effort and process, not just solutions.

Cultural Perspectives on Problem-Solving

In some cultures, adults traditionally provide solutions, while in others, children are expected to experiment more independently. A balanced approach—respecting cultural values while gradually empowering children to think for themselves—builds both respect and independence.

A Parent's Inner Challenge

Teaching problem-solving requires patience. It is often quicker for parents to decide, fix, or command. But speed sacrifices growth. The challenge is resisting the urge to solve every problem and instead trusting the child's capacity to learn.

Parents can reflect:

- "Do I give answers too quickly instead of asking questions?"
- "Do I value perfection over effort?"
- "Am I modeling problem-solving in my own life?"

Awareness shifts parents from rescuers to coaches.

Long-Term Benefits of Problem-Solving Skills

Children who learn problem-solving early grow into adults who:

- Face challenges with confidence.
- Persist through setbacks.
- Think creatively in school, work, and relationships.
- Resolve conflicts constructively.
- Develop independence and leadership.

Children who do not learn problem-solving may avoid responsibility, rely on others excessively, or collapse under pressure.

Final Takeaway

Problem-solving is one of the most valuable life skills a child can learn. Teaching it early equips children not just to follow rules but to think critically, act responsibly, and approach challenges with confidence. Parents who coach problem-solving create a foundation for resilience, independence, and creativity. In the end, every conflict, mistake, or challenge becomes an opportunity to grow. By teaching problem-solving early, parents are not only shaping childhood but preparing their children for a lifetime of strength and adaptability.

Role of Failure in Building Confidence

Parents naturally want to protect their children from disappointment. It can feel painful to watch a child fail—whether it's missing a goal in soccer, stumbling through a school presentation, or struggling to solve a math problem. The instinct to rescue is strong: stepping in to fix the problem, soften the blow, or shield them from defeat. Yet this instinct, though loving, can unintentionally rob children of one of life's greatest teachers: failure.

Failure is not the opposite of success—it is a critical part of it. Every inventor, leader, and achiever has failed repeatedly. Children who learn to face failure, recover, and try again grow into confident adults who persevere in the face of challenges. Children shielded from failure, or punished harshly for it, may fear risk, avoid responsibility, or collapse at the first setback.

The role of failure in building confidence cannot be overstated. It is in the moments of defeat that children discover their resilience, creativity, and strength.

Why Failure Matters

Failure offers unique lessons no success can provide:

- **Resilience:** Learning that setbacks are temporary and surmountable.
- **Humility:** Understanding that effort, not entitlement, earns achievement.
- **Adaptability:** Developing flexibility to adjust strategies when things don't work.
- **Confidence:** Building trust in one's ability to recover and try again.

When parents reframe failure as feedback rather than disaster, children begin to see mistakes as stepping stones instead of stumbling blocks.

The Science of Learning Through Failure

Neuroscience shows that the brain learns more from errors than from successes. When a child fails, their brain detects the error, adjusts, and strengthens new neural pathways for future attempts. Psychologists call this process "productive failure." Instead of discouragement, failure becomes fuel for growth.

Carol Dweck's research on growth mindset reinforces this. Children who believe abilities grow through effort interpret failure as an opportunity to learn. Those with fixed mindsets see failure as proof of inadequacy. Parents' responses to failure largely determine which mindset children adopt.

Real-World Example: The Spelling Bee

A child studies hard for a spelling bee but is eliminated in the second round.

Scenario A: The parent says, *"I can't believe you got out so early. You didn't practice enough."* The child feels ashamed and avoids trying again.

Scenario B: The parent says, *"I know you're disappointed. You worked hard, and that effort matters. What word tripped you up? Let's learn it together."* The child feels supported, reflects, and may enter again with renewed confidence.

In the second scenario, failure becomes a lesson, not a wound.

The Parent's Role in Framing Failure

Parents shape children's relationship with failure through their words and actions:

- **Normalize Mistakes:** Share personal failures openly: *"I once failed a test too, but I studied differently next time."*
- **Avoid Shame:** Correct actions without labeling the child. *"That didn't work,"* not *"You're a failure."*
- **Highlight Effort:** Praise persistence rather than only outcomes.
- **Encourage Reflection:** Ask, *"What did you learn from this? What could you try next time?"*

When parents treat failure as a teacher, children learn to do the same.

Allowing Small Failures Early

It may be tempting to fix every problem—bringing forgotten homework to school, tying shoes when a child struggles, or smoothing over playground disputes. But these small failures are safe training grounds. Experiencing manageable setbacks builds frustration tolerance, problem-solving, and accountability. Shielding children from failure leaves them unprepared for life's bigger challenges.

Balancing Support and Independence

Parents should not abandon children to failure but guide them through it. This balance means:

- Offering encouragement without rescuing.
- Providing tools for reflection and growth.
- Remaining emotionally present, so children feel supported even in defeat.

The message becomes: *"I believe in your ability to recover. You are not alone."*

Teaching Through Famous Failures

Stories of well-known figures illustrate the power of failure:

- **Thomas Edison** famously said, *"I have not failed. I've just found 10,000 ways that won't work."*
- **Michael Jordan** was cut from his high school basketball team but became one of the greatest athletes of all time.
- **J.K. Rowling** faced multiple rejections before publishing the *Harry Potter* series.

These examples show children that failure is not final—it is formative.

Failure and Emotional Regulation

Failure often triggers strong emotions: disappointment, embarrassment, anger. Teaching children to regulate these feelings is part of the process. Parents can coach them through calming strategies—breathing, naming emotions, taking breaks—before reflecting on lessons. This helps children separate the feeling of failure from their identity.

Real-World Example: The Science Fair

A child's science project collapses the morning of the fair.

Scenario A: The parent rushes to rebuild it while the child watches. The project is fixed, but the child learns helplessness.

Scenario B: The parent says, *"This is frustrating. Let's see what we can salvage. You can explain the process, even if the model isn't perfect."* The child learns adaptability and confidence in their own ability to handle setbacks.

The second approach transforms disaster into resilience.

Avoiding Common Pitfalls

- **Overprotecting:** Rescuing children from every failure prevents growth.
- **Overreacting:** Responding with anger or shame makes children fear mistakes.
- **Ignoring Effort:** Focusing only on results discourages persistence.
- **Equating Failure with Identity:** Saying, *"You failed,"* instead of, *"That attempt didn't work."*

Cultural Perspectives on Failure

Different cultures view failure differently. Some emphasize perfection and see mistakes as dishonor, while others embrace failure as part of learning. Parents can balance cultural expectations with the reality that failure is universal and essential. Teaching children to handle it with resilience prepares them for success in diverse environments.

A Parent's Inner Challenge

Parents' own relationship with failure deeply influences their responses. Adults raised in environments where mistakes were punished may fear letting children fail. Others may project their own anxieties, interpreting a child's failure as their own.

Reflective questions include:

- "How do I handle my own failures?"
- "Do I see mistakes as opportunities or disasters?"
- "Do I value effort as much as achievement?"

Working through these questions helps parents model a healthier relationship with failure.

Long-Term Benefits of Facing Failure

Children who are allowed to fail and supported through it develop:

- **Confidence:** Trust in their ability to recover.
- **Resilience:** Ability to handle setbacks without giving up.
- **Growth Mindset:** Belief that effort leads to improvement.
- **Problem-Solving:** Skills to adapt strategies when things don't work.
- **Courage:** Willingness to take risks and pursue goals despite uncertainty.

In contrast, children shielded from failure may become anxious, risk-averse, or dependent on others. Those punished harshly for failure may become perfectionists, fearful of mistakes, or rebellious.

Final Takeaway

Failure is not the end of confidence but the beginning of it. Every setback, mistake, or disappointment carries the seeds of growth. When parents allow children to fail safely, frame failure as feedback, and guide them toward reflection and persistence, they raise resilient, confident individuals. Protecting children from failure may ease short-term discomfort, but it steals long-term strength. Embracing failure as a teacher equips children with the courage to face life's challenges head-on.

Encouraging Self-Control and Patience

In a world of instant gratification—where snacks, screens, and entertainment are available at the tap of a button—self-control and patience are harder to teach than ever. Yet these two traits are among the most powerful predictors of long-term success. Children who learn to pause before acting, delay gratification, and wait calmly for what they want are better equipped to thrive in school, relationships, and life.

Self-control and patience are not about suppressing emotions or desires. They are about managing impulses, making thoughtful choices, and tolerating the discomfort of waiting. These skills form the backbone of resilience, responsibility, and maturity. Encouraging them in children requires intentional guidance, consistent practice, and plenty of modeling from parents.

Why Self-Control and Patience Matter

Decades of research highlight the importance of these skills:

- **The Marshmallow Test:** In the famous experiment by Walter Mischel, preschoolers were given a choice—eat one marshmallow now or wait and get two later. The children who waited demonstrated stronger academic performance, healthier relationships, and greater life satisfaction years later.
- **Academic Success:** Self-control predicts academic achievement better than IQ in many studies. Children who can manage distractions and persist through boring tasks complete homework, study effectively, and perform better.
- **Emotional Health:** Patience helps children manage frustration, reduce stress, and build healthier coping mechanisms.
- **Social Skills:** Children with self-control listen better, cooperate with peers, and build stronger friendships.

Without these skills, children may struggle with impulsivity, poor decision-making, or difficulty managing stress.

The Science Behind Self-Control

Self-control is largely governed by the prefrontal cortex, the brain region responsible for decision-making and impulse regulation. This area develops slowly, not reaching maturity until the mid-twenties. Children, therefore, are not naturally patient—they must be taught and guided.

Repeated practice with waiting, calming, and reflecting strengthens the brain's regulatory circuits. Over time, what begins as external guidance from parents becomes internal self-discipline.

Real-World Example: Waiting for Dessert

A child demands dessert immediately after dinner.

Scenario A: The parent caves: *"Fine, here's your cookie."* The child learns that impatience is rewarded.
Scenario B: The parent says sharply: *"Stop whining! You'll get dessert when I say so."* The child complies but feels resentful.
Scenario C: The parent says calmly: *"Dessert comes after dishes are cleared. You can choose to help me, and we'll get to it sooner."* The child learns both patience and the value of cooperation.

Only the third scenario builds self-control and patience in a constructive way.

How to Teach Self-Control and Patience

1. **Start Small:** Begin with short waiting periods, gradually increasing as children grow. For example, "Wait two minutes before snack" can become "Wait until after dinner."
2. **Use Visual Timers:** Young children struggle with abstract time. Timers, countdowns, or sandglasses make waiting concrete.
3. **Model Patience:** Parents who demonstrate calm waiting—at traffic lights, in long lines, or while cooking—teach through example.
4. **Practice Turn-Taking:** Board games and family routines that require waiting turns are natural practice for patience.
5. **Offer Praise for Waiting:** Acknowledge effort: *"I noticed you waited calmly for your turn. That shows great self-control."*
6. **Teach Calming Strategies:** Deep breaths, counting, or engaging in small distractions help children manage waiting without meltdown.

7. **Provide Choices During Waits:** *"While we wait for dinner, do you want to set the table or read a book?"*

Encouraging Reflection

When children succeed in waiting or controlling impulses, reflection cements the lesson. Ask: *"How did it feel to wait?"* or *"What helped you stay calm?"* Reflection shifts patience from something endured to a skill mastered.

The Role of Delayed Gratification

Teaching children that waiting brings greater rewards builds long-term motivation. Instead of immediate satisfaction, they learn to value persistence. Parents can structure opportunities for delayed gratification:

- Saving allowance for a bigger toy instead of buying small items immediately.
- Working toward family outings by completing chores consistently.
- Practicing for a recital or game with the promise of the pride that follows effort.

Each experience builds the understanding: effort + patience = greater reward.

Handling Impulsivity

Some children are naturally more impulsive, especially those with high energy or conditions like ADHD. For them, patience requires extra coaching. Strategies include:

- Clear, simple instructions.
- Shorter waiting periods with gradual extension.
- Physical outlets for energy while waiting.
- Visual reminders of progress ("three stars until game time").

Consistency is key—small, repeated successes build momentum.

Real-World Example: The Toy Store

A child wants a toy at the store.

Scenario A: The parent says, *"No, stop asking!"* and drags the child out, leading to tears and power struggles.
Scenario B: The parent says, *"We can't buy it today, but if you save your allowance, you can buy it in two weeks."* The child feels empowered, learns to plan, and practices patience.

The second approach uses a frustrating situation to build long-term skills.

Avoiding Common Pitfalls

- **Inconsistency:** If patience is rewarded sometimes and not others, children learn to push harder.
- **Excessive Harshness:** Demanding patience without support creates resentment.
- **Immediate Rewards:** Overusing instant gratification (like handing over a phone to stop whining) undermines self-control.
- **Unrealistic Expectations:** Expecting long patience from very young children sets them up for failure.

A Parent's Inner Challenge

Encouraging patience requires parents to model it—and that can be difficult in stressful lives. Parents who rush, lose temper quickly, or indulge impulsively may unintentionally undermine lessons. Reflective questions include:

- "How do I handle waiting in my own life?"
- "Do I model calm self-control or frustration?"
- "Am I consistent in rewarding patience?"

Children learn best from what parents show, not just what they say.

Long-Term Benefits

Children who master self-control and patience grow into adults who:

- Make thoughtful decisions instead of impulsive ones.
- Persist through long-term goals, from education to careers.
- Build stronger relationships through respect and cooperation.
- Handle stress with resilience and calm.
- Experience greater life satisfaction by valuing effort and achievement over instant gratification.

Without these skills, children risk impulsivity, poor decision-making, and difficulty managing frustration.

Final Takeaway

Self-control and patience are not innate—they are cultivated through practice, modeling, and consistent guidance. Parents who encourage these skills equip their children to face life's inevitable delays, obstacles, and challenges with resilience. In a world that prizes speed and instant gratification, teaching patience is an act of courage. It prepares children not just to succeed but to thrive—with calm, confidence, and strength.

Mindfulness and Calming Techniques for Kids

Modern childhood is filled with stimulation and stress. Screens flash constantly, school demands pile up, and social interactions bring both joy and conflict. For many children, emotions often feel too big to manage—anger that erupts in tantrums, anxiety that prevents sleep, or excitement that turns into restlessness. Parents long for strategies to help children find balance. One of the most effective tools is mindfulness and other calming techniques.

Mindfulness is simply the practice of paying attention to the present moment with curiosity and without judgment. For children, this skill builds self-awareness, emotional regulation, and resilience. Combined with calming techniques—such as breathing, visualization, or grounding exercises—mindfulness empowers children to manage stress and navigate emotions more effectively.

Why Mindfulness Matters for Children

Mindfulness is not just for adults. Research shows children who practice it experience:

- **Improved Attention:** Greater focus in school and activities.
- **Emotional Regulation:** Better management of anger, fear, or sadness.
- **Reduced Anxiety:** Lower stress levels and calmer responses to challenges.
- **Greater Empathy:** Increased ability to understand and respond to others' feelings.
- **Resilience:** Faster recovery from setbacks and frustrations.

In short, mindfulness strengthens both academic performance and emotional well-being.

The Science Behind Mindfulness

Neuroscience reveals that mindfulness strengthens the prefrontal cortex and reduces activity in the amygdala, the brain's fear center. This means children who practice mindfulness are better able to pause, think, and choose responses rather than reacting impulsively. Just as exercise strengthens muscles, mindfulness strengthens the brain's ability to stay calm under pressure.

Real-World Example: The Test-Day Jitters

A child feels anxious before a school test.

Scenario A: The parent says, *"Don't worry, you'll be fine."* The child still feels anxious and unprepared.
Scenario B: The parent guides the child through deep breaths: *"Breathe in slowly through your nose, out through your mouth. Focus on your breath."* The child's heart rate slows, and calm replaces panic.

The second approach gives the child a tool, not just reassurance.

Simple Mindfulness Practices for Kids

Mindfulness doesn't require long meditation sessions. Short, playful practices work best for children:

1. **Mindful Breathing:** Teach children to notice their breath. Use imagery: *"Smell the flower, blow the candle."* This helps anchor attention.
2. **Body Scan:** Encourage children to close their eyes and notice each part of their body, from toes to head. Builds awareness and relaxation.
3. **Five Senses Check-In:** Ask children to notice five things they see, four they feel, three they hear, two they smell, one they taste. This grounds them in the present.
4. **Glitter Jar:** Shake a jar with glitter and water. As the glitter settles, explain it's like their thoughts and feelings calming down. Watching the jar helps them slow their minds.
5. **Mindful Eating:** Have children eat a raisin or small snack slowly, noticing texture, taste, and smell. This teaches focus and appreciation.
6. **Nature Walks:** Encourage noticing sounds, colors, and textures outside. Mindfulness blends naturally with exploration.

Calming Techniques for Emotional Regulation

Mindfulness pairs well with calming strategies for moments of intense emotion:

- **Counting Breaths:** Count slowly to three while inhaling and three while exhaling.
- **Progressive Muscle Relaxation:** Tense and relax muscles one by one.
- **Visualization:** Imagine a safe, calm place, like a beach or cozy room.
- **Grounding Techniques:** Touch an object, notice its texture, or press feet into the floor to reconnect with the present.
- **Movement:** Yoga poses, stretching, or slow walking calm both body and mind.

These techniques give children practical tools to manage overwhelming feelings.

Integrating Mindfulness Into Daily Life

Parents can make mindfulness part of everyday routines:

- A breathing exercise before bed.
- A gratitude reflection at dinner.
- A mindful pause in the car before school.
- A family "quiet minute" to reset during busy days.

Consistency matters more than duration. A few minutes daily builds lasting habits.

Real-World Example: The After-School Meltdown

A child storms home, upset about a playground conflict.

Scenario A: The parent lectures immediately: *"You shouldn't yell at your friends."* The child resists, still overwhelmed.

Scenario B: The parent says, *"Let's sit together and take three breaths first. Then you can tell me what happened."* The child calms enough to reflect and talk through the conflict.

The mindful pause opens space for constructive conversation.

Mindfulness in Schools

Many schools now incorporate mindfulness into classrooms, with practices like breathing breaks, meditation apps, or mindful listening exercises. Studies show these programs reduce bullying, improve focus, and increase kindness. Parents who reinforce mindfulness at home extend these benefits.

Avoiding Misconceptions

Some parents worry mindfulness is too abstract, too "adult," or even spiritual. In reality, mindfulness for children is practical, playful, and secular. It is not about emptying the mind but about paying attention with curiosity. Children already live in the moment—mindfulness teaches them to notice and manage that experience.

A Parent's Inner Challenge

Parents' own stress levels often interfere with teaching calm. It is hard to guide mindfulness when feeling rushed or overwhelmed. In fact, children often mirror parents' states. Practicing mindfulness together can help both parent and child.

Reflective questions for parents:

- "Do I model calmness or constant stress?"
- "Do I rush to fix emotions instead of pausing to breathe with my child?"
- "Am I willing to learn mindfulness alongside my child?"

Mindfulness becomes a family practice, not just a child's lesson.

Long-Term Benefits of Mindfulness

Children who practice mindfulness develop:

- **Emotional Intelligence:** Awareness and regulation of feelings.
- **Resilience:** Ability to recover from stress and setbacks.
- **Focus:** Greater attention in school and tasks.
- **Empathy:** Stronger understanding of others' perspectives.
- **Calm Confidence:** Trust in their ability to manage emotions.

Without these skills, children may grow more reactive, anxious, or overwhelmed by life's challenges.

Final Takeaway

Mindfulness and calming techniques are not luxuries—they are life skills. In a world of constant distraction and pressure, they give children the tools to pause, breathe, and respond with clarity. Parents who integrate mindfulness into daily routines raise children who are not only calmer in the moment but also more resilient, empathetic, and confident for life. Helping children center themselves in the present prepares them to face the future with balance and strength.

CHAPTER 7

Empowering Independence and Confidence

Giving Kids Choices That Matter

Every child, from toddlerhood to adolescence, has a deep need for autonomy. They want to feel that their voice matters, that their actions influence outcomes, and that they are not simply passive recipients of adult control. Parents often hear children declare, *"I can do it myself!"* or *"You're not the boss of me!"* These statements, while sometimes exasperating, reflect a natural and healthy drive for independence.

Yet giving children choices does not mean handing over full control or indulging every whim. The art of parenting lies in offering choices that empower children while still maintaining structure. When done well, offering meaningful choices fosters responsibility, confidence, and decision-making skills. When neglected, children may feel powerless, leading to defiance—or conversely, overly dependent on others to decide for them.

The key is giving choices that matter—decisions appropriate to a child's age, within safe boundaries, and with real consequences.

Why Choices Matter

Psychological research consistently shows that autonomy is a core human need. Self-determination theory, developed by psychologists Edward Deci and Richard Ryan, emphasizes that autonomy, competence, and connection are essential for motivation and well-being. Children who feel they have some control over their lives are more engaged, cooperative, and resilient.

When parents give children choices, they:

- **Strengthen Confidence:** Children trust their ability to make decisions.
- **Teach Responsibility:** Choices come with consequences that build accountability.

- **Reduce Power Struggles:** Offering structured choices turns battles into collaboration.
- **Encourage Independence:** Children learn to rely on their own judgment, preparing for adulthood.

The Difference Between Real and False Choices

Children quickly sense when choices are meaningless. Offering false choices—*"Do you want broccoli or broccoli?"*—creates frustration rather than empowerment. Real choices involve genuine options with distinct outcomes. However, too much freedom, like *"Do whatever you want,"* overwhelms children and creates chaos.

The balance lies in structured choices: clear, limited options within boundaries set by parents.

Real-World Example: The Morning Routine

A child resists getting dressed for school.

Scenario A: The parent commands: *"Put on these clothes now!"* The child refuses, leading to a power struggle.
Scenario B: The parent offers a choice: *"Do you want to wear the blue shirt or the red one?"* The child feels empowered and cooperates.

The difference is not about clothing but about autonomy. The child learns they have a voice within limits.

How to Offer Choices That Matter

1. **Limit Options:** Two or three choices are enough. Too many create overwhelm.
2. **Ensure Both Options Are Acceptable:** Parents should be comfortable with either choice.

3. **Connect Choices to Responsibility:** Emphasize that choices bring consequences. *"If you choose not to do homework now, you'll need to do it before playtime."*
4. **Offer Age-Appropriate Decisions:** Younger children choose clothing or snacks; older children choose extracurriculars or study strategies.
5. **Respect Their Decision:** Once chosen, resist overriding unless safety is at risk.

Choices That Grow With Age

- **Toddlers:** Simple, concrete choices. *"Do you want the red cup or the blue cup?"*
- **Elementary Children:** Choices involving responsibility. *"Do you want to do homework before or after snack?"*
- **Preteens:** Choices about hobbies, activities, and schedules.
- **Teenagers:** Increasingly significant choices about academics, friendships, and future goals—with parental guidance rather than control.

Gradually expanding choices helps children practice independence safely.

Teaching Through Consequences

Choices matter most when children experience their outcomes. If a child chooses not to wear a coat, they feel cold (as long as safety isn't compromised). If a teenager chooses to procrastinate, they face the stress of last-minute work. Parents should resist rescuing from every consequence—natural outcomes are powerful teachers.

Real-World Example: The Sleepover Decision

A preteen asks to attend a sleepover.

Scenario A: The parent decides unilaterally: *"No, you're not going."* The child feels powerless and resentful.

Scenario B: The parent discusses: *"It's your choice, but think about how you'll feel tomorrow with a sports game after little sleep."* The child reflects, weighing pros and cons, and makes a decision.

In the second scenario, the parent still guides but leaves space for autonomy.

Avoiding Common Pitfalls

- **Too Many Choices:** Overwhelms children and causes indecision.
- **No Real Authority:** Allowing unsafe or inappropriate choices undermines parental guidance.
- **Rescuing From Consequences:** Protecting children from outcomes weakens accountability.
- **False Choices:** Pretending to offer options when none exist erodes trust.

Empowering Without Overindulging

Some parents, eager to empower, hand over too much control. Allowing children to dictate bedtimes, meals, or financial decisions creates chaos and entitlement. Balance is key—parents remain guides, not dictators, but also not passive observers.

A Parent's Inner Challenge

Offering choices can feel slower and more complicated than giving orders. Parents in a rush may default to commands. Others may fear losing control if too many decisions are handed over. Yet investing in choices pays off—children learn responsibility now, reducing conflicts later.

Reflective questions for parents:

- "Do I offer real choices or only token ones?"
- "Do I step in too quickly instead of letting my child decide?"
- "Am I willing to let my child face small consequences to learn accountability?"

These reflections help parents find the right balance between guidance and autonomy.

Long-Term Benefits of Choices That Matter

Children who grow up with meaningful choices develop:

- **Confidence:** Trust in their ability to make decisions.
- **Independence:** Reduced dependence on others for direction.
- **Accountability:** Understanding that choices carry consequences.
- **Critical Thinking:** Skills in weighing options and outcomes.
- **Healthy Relationships:** Respect for their own voice and the voices of others.

By contrast, children raised with no choices may become dependent or defiant, while those raised with excessive freedom may become entitled or reckless.

Final Takeaway

Giving children choices that matter is not about indulging or abandoning guidance. It is about striking a balance—offering structured freedom within safe boundaries. Each choice becomes a practice round for adulthood, where decisions carry weight and consequences. Parents who provide meaningful choices raise children who are confident, responsible, and prepared for independence. In the end, empowering children with choices is not about giving up authority but about teaching them to use their own wisely.

Encouraging Decision-Making and Ownership

Every day, children face decisions: what to wear, how to spend free time, whether to share a toy, or how to handle conflict. While many of these seem small, each is a rehearsal for the larger decisions they will face as adults—choosing friends, setting priorities, managing money, and eventually, building careers and families. Parents who encourage decision-making and ownership equip their children with one of the most essential life skills: the ability to choose wisely and accept responsibility for those choices.

Too often, parents make decisions for children in the name of efficiency, protection, or control. While this may reduce mistakes in the short term, it undermines confidence and independence in the long term. Children who never practice decision-making may grow into adults who avoid responsibility, look to others for direction, or fear risk. Conversely, children who are given opportunities to decide, reflect, and own their outcomes develop confidence, accountability, and resilience.

Why Decision-Making Matters

Decision-making teaches children to:

- **Think Critically:** Weigh options, evaluate consequences, and make informed choices.
- **Build Confidence:** Trust their ability to act and learn from outcomes.
- **Accept Responsibility:** Recognize that choices shape results.
- **Develop Independence:** Reduce reliance on parents or peers for direction.
- **Strengthen Resilience:** Learn that mistakes are part of growth, not reasons to give up.

Ownership turns decision-making into growth. When children take ownership, they don't just make choices—they stand behind them, learn from them, and adapt next time.

The Psychology of Choice and Control

Research shows that a sense of control increases motivation and resilience. Psychologists call this an "internal locus of control"—the belief that one's actions influence outcomes. Children with an internal locus of control tend to persist through challenges, while those with an external locus (believing luck, fate, or others determine outcomes) are more likely to give up or blame others.

Encouraging decision-making and ownership nurtures an internal locus of control, empowering children to see themselves as capable agents of their lives.

Real-World Example: The Missed Assignment

A middle schooler forgets to complete a project.

Scenario A: The parent takes over, completing parts of it to ensure a good grade. The child learns dependence and avoids responsibility. Scenario B: The parent says, *"You'll need to talk to your teacher and explain what happened. What's your plan to fix it?"* The child takes ownership, faces the consequence, and learns accountability.

Only the second scenario builds decision-making and ownership.

Teaching the Decision-Making Process

Decision-making is a skill that can be broken into steps:

1. **Identify the Decision:** Name the choice clearly. *"Do I spend allowance now or save it?"*
2. **Consider Options:** Brainstorm possible choices.

3. **Weigh Consequences:** Discuss what might happen with each choice.
4. **Make the Decision:** Choose confidently.
5. **Take Ownership:** Accept responsibility for the outcome.
6. **Reflect and Learn:** Afterward, ask, *"What worked? What would I do differently?"*

This process transforms impulsive choices into thoughtful ones.

Age-Appropriate Decision-Making

- **Toddlers:** Simple, concrete choices. *"Do you want an apple or a banana?"*
- **Elementary Children:** Daily routines and responsibilities. *"Do you want to do homework before or after snack?"*
- **Preteens:** Choices about hobbies, friendships, and schedules.
- **Teenagers:** Increasingly complex decisions about academics, money, and social life—with parents offering guidance but not control.

Gradual expansion allows children to practice decision-making safely.

Encouraging Ownership Through Consequences

Children learn ownership when they experience the results of their choices. Parents who rescue too quickly undermine learning. For example:

- If a child forgets a jacket, feeling cold teaches more than a lecture.
- If a teen oversleeps, facing the consequences at school is more instructive than a parent making excuses.

Natural and logical consequences reinforce ownership better than punishment.

Real-World Example: The Sports Team

A teenager considers quitting a sports team mid-season.

Scenario A: The parent decides: *"You signed up, so you're quitting now."* The teen feels controlled, not responsible.
Scenario B: The parent says: *"This is your decision. But think about how quitting affects your teammates. What do you want to do?"* The teen reflects, weighs consequences, and chooses—owning the outcome.

Guidance plus autonomy builds maturity.

Avoiding Common Pitfalls

- **Over-Controlling:** Making all decisions teaches dependence.
- **Over-Indulging:** Allowing unsafe or inappropriate decisions undermines guidance.
- **Rescuing From Consequences:** Protecting children from results weakens ownership.
- **Shaming Mistakes:** Turning poor decisions into humiliation discourages risk-taking.

Modeling Decision-Making

Parents teach most powerfully through example. Narrating decisions—*"I'm choosing to cook at home instead of ordering out because it saves money"*—shows children the process of weighing options and taking ownership. Sharing mistakes openly models reflection: *"I didn't plan well today, and I ran out of time. Next time, I'll start earlier."*

Building Confidence Through Mistakes

Mistakes are inevitable, but they are also powerful teachers. Parents should normalize failure as part of decision-making. Instead of saying, *"You made a bad choice,"* they can say, *"That choice didn't work out. What can you do differently?"* This reframing encourages learning rather than fear.

A Parent's Inner Challenge

Parents often struggle with giving up control. Allowing children to decide means allowing them to make mistakes—and watching those mistakes can be uncomfortable. Reflective questions include:

- "Do I trust my child enough to let them decide?"
- "Do I step in too quickly to prevent discomfort?"
- "Am I modeling ownership in my own decisions?"

The challenge is not about relinquishing all control but about creating space for growth.

Long-Term Benefits of Decision-Making and Ownership

Children raised with decision-making opportunities and ownership develop:

- **Confidence:** Belief in their ability to handle challenges.
- **Independence:** Reduced reliance on peers or parents for direction.
- **Accountability:** Willingness to own mistakes and learn.
- **Critical Thinking:** Skills to evaluate options and foresee consequences.
- **Resilience:** Ability to recover from poor decisions and try again.

By contrast, children shielded from decisions may grow indecisive, passive, or easily swayed by peers.

Final Takeaway

Encouraging decision-making and ownership is one of the most important ways parents prepare children for adulthood. It is not about control or indulgence but about balance—guiding children while giving them space to choose, fail, learn, and grow. Each decision, whether small or significant, is practice for a future where ownership and accountability are essential. Parents who nurture this skill raise children who are confident, independent, and resilient—ready to shape their own lives with wisdom and courage.

Nurturing Talents and Unique Strengths

Every child comes into the world with a unique blend of abilities, interests, and potential. Some shine early through art, music, or sports. Others reveal their gifts more quietly—through empathy, problem-solving, leadership, or creativity in play. Too often, however, children's unique strengths are overlooked in favor of standardized measures of success: test scores, grades, or conformity to societal expectations.

Nurturing talents and strengths is not about grooming a child for fame or forcing them toward a career path. It is about recognizing what makes them unique, celebrating it, and creating opportunities for growth. When children feel their strengths are seen and valued, they gain confidence, motivation, and resilience. They learn that their individuality is not something to hide but something to cultivate.

Why Strength-Based Parenting Matters

Traditional parenting often focuses on fixing weaknesses: the poor grade in math, the lack of focus in sports, the messy handwriting. While addressing challenges is important, an exclusive focus on weaknesses can undermine confidence. Children may internalize the message that they are never "good enough."

Strength-based parenting flips this perspective. It emphasizes identifying and nurturing what children do well, then using those strengths as foundations for growth. Research by psychologist Lea Waters highlights that strength-based parenting boosts self-esteem, academic achievement, and emotional well-being.

Children raised in environments where strengths are valued develop:

- **Confidence:** Belief in their abilities.
- **Motivation:** Drive to pursue passions.
- **Resilience:** Ability to recover from setbacks by leaning on strengths.
- **Identity:** A sense of who they are and what makes them valuable.

Recognizing Talents and Strengths

Strengths are not always obvious. Some children display them boldly; others reveal them quietly over time. Parents can look for:

- **Flow Moments:** Times when children are deeply absorbed and lose track of time.
- **Ease of Learning:** Skills that come naturally with little instruction.
- **Joyful Engagement:** Activities that bring visible excitement and energy.
- **Consistent Interest:** Patterns of curiosity or practice, even without external reward.

Talents may emerge in unexpected ways: a knack for storytelling, compassion for animals, or leadership in group play. Parents must observe carefully, resisting the urge to compare siblings or peers.

Real-World Example: The Budding Artist

A child doodles constantly in class and at home.

Scenario A: The parent scolds, *"Stop wasting time and focus on real work."* The child learns to suppress their passion.
Scenario B: The parent says, *"I see how much you enjoy drawing. Let's find an art class where you can explore more."* The child feels validated and motivated, building confidence through their talent.

The second scenario nurtures both skill and self-worth.

Creating Opportunities for Growth

Once strengths are identified, parents can create opportunities to nurture them:

1. **Provide Resources:** Books, classes, mentors, or tools related to their interest.
2. **Encourage Practice:** Support regular, enjoyable practice without pressure.
3. **Celebrate Progress:** Acknowledge growth and effort, not just achievement.
4. **Connect Strengths to Values:** Show how strengths can serve others. A child good at organizing might help plan family events.
5. **Balance Exploration:** Encourage trying multiple interests before narrowing too early.

Avoiding Pressure and Perfectionism

Parents sometimes push too hard once a talent is identified, turning passion into pressure. Over-scheduling, constant critique, or unrealistic expectations can cause burnout. Children may lose joy in their strength or feel defined solely by performance.

The goal is to support without suffocating. Encouragement should foster love of learning, not fear of failure.

Real-World Example: The Young Musician

A child shows talent in piano.

Scenario A: The parent demands hours of practice daily, criticizes mistakes, and pressures for competitions. The child grows resentful and quits.
Scenario B: The parent encourages regular practice, celebrates progress, and offers performance opportunities when the child is ready. The child enjoys music, builds skill, and persists long term.

Balance is key: nurturing without overwhelming.

Building Strengths into Everyday Life

Talents should not exist only in structured lessons—they can be woven into daily routines. A child with storytelling talent might read bedtime stories to siblings. A child skilled in problem-solving might help plan the grocery budget. Integrating strengths into family life reinforces value and usefulness.

Helping Children See Their Own Strengths

Children often downplay their abilities, comparing themselves to peers. Parents can help by:

- Pointing out specific strengths: *"You're really good at calming your brother when he's upset."*
- Encouraging reflection: *"What was your favorite part of today? What made you feel proud?"*
- Sharing observations from others: teachers, coaches, or family members.

Hearing strengths named builds self-awareness and pride.

Using Strengths to Address Weaknesses

Strengths can be leveraged to support weaker areas. For example:

- A child strong in creativity might use drawing to make math problems more engaging.
- A child strong in leadership might be paired with peers to boost teamwork skills.
- A child with persistence in sports might transfer that determination to academics.

This approach reframes challenges as opportunities for strengths to shine.

A Parent's Inner Challenge

Parents' own expectations and insecurities often shape how they nurture strengths. Some may project their unfulfilled dreams onto children, pushing them toward talents they themselves desired. Others may dismiss talents that don't fit traditional definitions of success.

Reflective questions for parents:

- "Do I value my child's strengths, even if they differ from my own?"
- "Am I supporting growth, or pushing performance for my pride?"
- "Do I celebrate effort, or only visible achievement?"

Honest reflection helps parents nurture authentically.

Long-Term Benefits of Nurturing Strengths

Children whose strengths are recognized and supported develop:

- **Confidence:** Trust in their unique abilities.

- **Resilience:** Ability to rely on strengths during setbacks.
- **Motivation:** Drive to pursue passions with energy.
- **Identity:** A sense of self rooted in individuality, not conformity.
- **Contribution:** Understanding that their gifts can serve others.

In contrast, children whose strengths are ignored or suppressed may feel invisible, unmotivated, or disconnected from their potential.

Final Takeaway

Every child has unique strengths waiting to be discovered. Parenting that nurtures these strengths builds not only talent but character, resilience, and confidence. The goal is not perfection or performance but empowerment—the belief that who they are matters and what they bring to the world is valuable. By nurturing talents and unique strengths, parents give children the courage to embrace themselves fully and the motivation to grow into the best version of who they can be.

Turning Mistakes Into Learning Experiences

Every child makes mistakes. They spill juice, forget homework, hurt a friend's feelings, or misjudge a situation. For parents, these moments can be frustrating, especially when the same mistakes happen repeatedly. Yet mistakes are not signs of failure—they are opportunities for growth. The way parents respond determines whether mistakes become sources of shame or stepping stones toward wisdom.

When children are punished harshly or shamed for mistakes, they often retreat into fear, avoidance, or dishonesty. They learn to hide errors rather than face them. When mistakes are embraced as natural and instructive, children develop resilience, accountability, and problem-solving skills. They learn that imperfection is part of learning and that growth often comes through failure.

Turning mistakes into learning experiences is about shifting perspective—from *"You failed"* to *"Here's what you can learn."* This shift transforms childhood challenges into lifelong strengths.

Why Mistakes Matter

Mistakes serve several developmental purposes:

- **They teach problem-solving.** Errors reveal what doesn't work, prompting new strategies.
- **They build resilience.** Recovering from mistakes shows children they can bounce back.
- **They normalize imperfection.** Children learn that everyone errs, reducing shame.
- **They foster accountability.** Owning mistakes builds integrity.
- **They encourage curiosity.** Children who see mistakes as learning opportunities explore more boldly.

Without mistakes, growth stalls. The fear of error can paralyze children, preventing them from trying new things or taking healthy risks.

The Science of Learning From Mistakes

Research shows that the brain learns more from failure than success. When children make a mistake, their brains generate error signals that adjust neural pathways. This process strengthens future performance. Psychologists call it "productive failure."

Carol Dweck's work on growth mindset reinforces this. Children who view mistakes as opportunities to improve are more motivated, persistent, and successful. Those who see mistakes as proof of inadequacy often give up. Parents play a pivotal role in shaping these mindsets.

Real-World Example: The Spilled Juice

A child knocks over a glass of juice at dinner.

Scenario A: The parent scolds: *"You're so careless! Why can't you pay attention?"* The child feels ashamed and fearful of trying again. Scenario B: The parent says: *"Spills happen. Let's grab a towel and clean it up. Next time, try holding the glass with both hands."* The child learns responsibility and strategy without shame.

The second response transforms a small mistake into a life lesson.

How to Turn Mistakes Into Learning

1. **Stay Calm:** Parents who react with anger turn mistakes into trauma. Calm responses open the door to learning.
2. **Acknowledge the Mistake:** Help the child recognize what happened without judgment.
3. **Encourage Reflection:** Ask, *"What went wrong? What could you do differently?"*
4. **Teach Strategies:** Offer guidance or tools for improvement.
5. **Allow Repair:** If the mistake hurt someone, encourage apologies and amends.
6. **Reinforce Effort:** Praise the courage to try again.

Balancing Accountability and Compassion

Accountability is crucial—children must recognize that mistakes have consequences. But accountability without compassion leads to shame. The balance is teaching children to own errors while also feeling supported. The message becomes: *"You are responsible, but you are not defined by mistakes."*

Real-World Example: The Forgotten Homework

A child forgets homework at school.

Scenario A: The parent yells, *"You're so irresponsible! No TV for a week!"* The child learns only fear.
Scenario B: The parent says: *"You forgot your homework. Tomorrow, what's one way you can remind yourself before leaving?"* The child reflects and develops strategies.

The second approach builds problem-solving and ownership.

Mistakes in Relationships

Not all mistakes are academic or practical; many involve relationships—hurting a sibling, losing patience with a friend, or speaking unkindly. These mistakes are particularly important for learning empathy and repair. Parents can guide children to:

- Recognize the harm caused.
- Apologize sincerely.
- Make amends through kind actions.

Learning to repair relationships builds both responsibility and emotional intelligence.

Avoiding Common Pitfalls

- **Shaming:** Attacking the child's character instead of addressing behavior.
- **Over-Rescuing:** Preventing mistakes or fixing them immediately robs children of learning.
- **Excessive Punishment:** Disproportionate consequences shift focus from reflection to fear.
- **Ignoring Patterns:** Failing to address repeated mistakes misses opportunities for growth.

Encouraging a Growth Mindset

Parents can foster growth mindset by reframing language:

- Instead of *"You're bad at math,"* say, *"You haven't mastered it yet."*
- Instead of *"You failed,"* say, *"This is a chance to learn."*
- Instead of *"Don't make mistakes,"* say, *"Mistakes are part of learning."*

These small shifts create environments where children feel safe to try, fail, and grow.

A Parent's Inner Challenge

Many parents struggle with mistakes because of their own upbringing. If they were punished harshly for errors, they may repeat the pattern. Others may overcompensate, rescuing children from discomfort. Reflection helps break these cycles:

- "Do I see mistakes as disasters or opportunities?"
- "Do I model learning from my own mistakes?"
- "Am I too quick to rescue or too quick to punish?"

Self-awareness helps parents respond with balance and wisdom.

Long-Term Benefits

Children raised to see mistakes as learning experiences develop:

- **Resilience:** Confidence to recover from setbacks.
- **Problem-Solving:** Skills to adapt strategies.
- **Accountability:** Willingness to own and repair errors.
- **Courage:** Willingness to take healthy risks.
- **Self-Compassion:** Ability to forgive themselves and keep trying.

In contrast, children raised with shame around mistakes may fear risk, avoid responsibility, or hide errors.

Final Takeaway

Mistakes are not failures but lessons. They are the raw material of growth, resilience, and wisdom. Parents who transform mistakes into learning opportunities teach children to see imperfection not as shameful but as natural and valuable. By responding with calm, compassion, and accountability, parents raise children who approach life with courage, curiosity, and confidence. In the end, mistakes are not setbacks—they are stepping stones to success.

Raising Leaders, Not Followers

Every parent hopes their child will grow into someone who stands tall, makes wise choices, and contributes positively to the world. Yet leadership is often misunderstood. Many imagine leaders as loud, authoritative figures commanding attention. In reality, leadership is less about being in charge and more about taking responsibility, showing integrity, and inspiring others. True leaders do not demand obedience—they earn respect.

Raising leaders does not mean grooming children to dominate or always be first. It means equipping them with the skills to think independently, act responsibly, and stand firm in their values. In a world filled with peer pressure, social media influence, and shifting cultural norms, children who learn leadership early are less likely to be swayed blindly. They become individuals who can chart their own path, encourage others, and solve problems with courage and compassion.

Why Leadership Matters in Childhood

Leadership skills developed in childhood extend far beyond the playground or classroom. Children who learn to lead:

- **Think Critically:** They evaluate situations instead of following blindly.
- **Stand Confidently:** They make choices aligned with values, not peer pressure.
- **Influence Positively:** They inspire and support others rather than dominate them.
- **Take Responsibility:** They own their actions and decisions.
- **Build Resilience:** They recover from setbacks and keep guiding themselves and others forward.

Raising leaders is not about ego—it is about equipping children with life skills that foster independence, responsibility, and integrity.

The Difference Between Leaders and Followers

- **Followers** often look to others for direction, avoiding responsibility when things go wrong. They may be swayed by popularity or fear of exclusion.
- **Leaders** take initiative, guide with respect, and stay true to values even when unpopular.

Children raised only to comply may become passive followers. Children raised with encouragement to think, decide, and act responsibly develop leadership qualities that prepare them for adulthood.

Real-World Example: The Playground Group

A group of children debates which game to play.

Scenario A: A child says, *"Let's just do what everyone else wants."* They avoid conflict but contribute little direction.
Scenario B: Another child says, *"We have two ideas: tag or soccer. Let's take a quick vote."* The group agrees and starts playing.

The second child demonstrates leadership—not by bossing others, but by facilitating fairness and action.

How Parents Can Raise Leaders

1. **Encourage Independent Thinking:** Ask children what they think before giving answers. *"What would you do in this situation?"*
2. **Model Integrity:** Show that leadership is about doing what's right, not what's easy.
3. **Provide Opportunities to Lead:** Allow children to make decisions for themselves, siblings, or group activities.
4. **Teach Empathy:** True leaders listen and consider others' needs.
5. **Normalize Mistakes:** Leaders stumble but recover. Encourage learning from errors.
6. **Praise Courage:** Acknowledge when children speak up or take initiative, even in small ways.

Leadership at Different Ages

- **Toddlers:** Practice leadership through simple choices—picking a snack or leading a cleanup song.
- **Elementary-Age Children:** Encourage taking turns leading games or helping with family decisions.
- **Preteens:** Support leadership in group projects, extracurricular activities, or community service.
- **Teenagers:** Encourage leadership roles in clubs, sports, or volunteering, while guiding reflection on values and responsibilities.

Gradual exposure to leadership opportunities allows confidence to grow naturally.

Balancing Leadership and Humility

Raising leaders does not mean creating bossy or arrogant children. True leadership balances confidence with humility. Parents can reinforce this by teaching:

- **Collaboration:** Leadership involves working with, not above, others.
- **Listening:** Great leaders listen as much as they speak.
- **Service:** Leadership is about lifting others, not just advancing oneself.

Real-World Example: The Group Project

A child works on a group project at school.

Scenario A: They take over completely, refusing input. The group resents them.
Scenario B: They assign roles fairly, encourage ideas, and help the group succeed.

The second scenario reflects true leadership—guiding without dominating.

Avoiding Common Pitfalls

- **Overemphasis on Winning:** Teaching children that leadership is about always being first creates pressure and arrogance.
- **Suppressing Initiative:** Dismissing children's ideas discourages leadership.
- **Rescuing Too Quickly:** Not allowing children to solve problems undermines initiative.
- **Equating Leadership With Personality:** Both introverts and extroverts can lead. Leadership is not about volume but vision and values.

A Parent's Inner Challenge

Parents' own beliefs about leadership often influence how they encourage it. Some may confuse leadership with control, pushing children to dominate. Others may discourage leadership, fearing arrogance or conflict. Reflective questions include:

- "Do I give my child space to lead, or do I control too tightly?"
- "Am I modeling leadership through responsibility and integrity?"
- "Do I value collaboration as much as independence?"

Self-awareness allows parents to guide leadership in healthy, balanced ways.

Long-Term Benefits of Raising Leaders

Children raised with leadership skills develop into adults who:

- Make independent, responsible choices.
- Resist peer pressure and societal manipulation.
- Influence others positively through empathy and integrity.
- Handle setbacks with resilience.
- Contribute to communities, workplaces, and relationships as proactive, responsible individuals.

By contrast, children raised only to follow may become passive, indecisive, or easily swayed.

Final Takeaway

Raising leaders is not about creating future CEOs or politicians. It is about instilling qualities of independence, responsibility, empathy, and courage. Leaders are those who think critically, act with integrity, and inspire others—not those who dominate. Parents who encourage leadership raise children who stand strong against pressure, make wise choices, and contribute positively to the world. In the end, the goal is not to raise followers who conform, but leaders who create, serve, and inspire.

CHAPTER 8

Parenting for the Long Term

Adapting Strategies as Children Grow

Parenting is not a static role. What works beautifully for a toddler often fails with a teenager. The strategies that soothe a preschool tantrum may only provoke an eye roll in middle school. Effective parenting requires constant adaptation—adjusting expectations, communication, and discipline as children move through stages of development.

Adapting strategies is not about being inconsistent; it is about being responsive. Just as teachers modify lessons for different grade levels, parents must adjust guidance for a child's age, maturity, and temperament. This flexibility shows respect for a child's growth and prepares them for the increasing independence of adulthood. Parents who fail to adapt may find themselves locked in power struggles or disconnected from their child's evolving needs.

Why Adaptation Matters

Children's brains, bodies, and emotions change rapidly. Parenting strategies that ignore these shifts can create friction. Adaptation matters because it:

- **Supports Development:** Aligns expectations with a child's capabilities.
- **Fosters Independence:** Gives children room to grow responsibly.
- **Strengthens Connection:** Shows respect for maturity and individuality.
- **Prevents Conflict:** Reduces frustration by adjusting guidance to fit the moment.

Parenting is not about control but about guidance. Adapting strategies ensures guidance evolves alongside the child.

Understanding Developmental Stages

Each stage of childhood presents unique challenges and opportunities:

- **Toddlers (1–3 years):** Need structure, safety, and clear boundaries. Strategies focus on routines, simple choices, and emotional labeling.
- **Preschoolers (3–5 years):** Develop imagination and social skills. Strategies emphasize play, storytelling, and guided sharing.
- **Elementary Years (6–11 years):** Build responsibility and competence. Strategies shift toward chores, problem-solving, and consistent accountability.
- **Adolescence (12–18 years):** Seek independence and identity. Strategies require respect, negotiation, and trust-building.

Adapting does not mean abandoning values but adjusting methods to fit the child's growth.

Real-World Example: Bedtime

A toddler resists bedtime. The parent reads a short story, offers comfort, and enforces a routine.
A ten-year-old resists bedtime. The parent sets consistent lights-out but allows some independence—perhaps choosing their own reading material before sleep.
A teenager resists bedtime. The parent discusses the importance of sleep, negotiates reasonable limits, and allows natural consequences of fatigue to reinforce responsibility.

The core principle—healthy rest—remains constant, but the strategy evolves.

From Control to Collaboration

Parenting young children often requires more control: setting limits, redirecting behavior, and enforcing rules. As children grow, strategies must shift toward collaboration—listening to opinions, involving them in decisions, and respecting autonomy.

For example, a toddler might be told, *"It's time to put toys away."* An older child might be asked, *"Would you like to clean up before dinner or after?"* A teenager might be part of setting the household rules: *"How can we make sure everyone contributes to chores fairly?"*

This progression respects maturity while still maintaining parental guidance.

The Role of Communication

Adapting strategies requires evolving communication.

- **With toddlers:** Use simple language and repetition.
- **With school-age children:** Use explanations and encourage questions.
- **With teenagers:** Use dialogue, respect, and listening more than lecturing.

Communication style grows with the child. What begins as instruction matures into conversation and, eventually, partnership.

Real-World Example: The Missed Curfew

A 7-year-old breaks a rule (watching TV after bedtime). The parent enforces consequences directly.
A 14-year-old breaks curfew. The parent holds a conversation: *"What happened? How can we rebuild trust?"* The consequence may involve reduced privileges, but the dialogue teaches accountability and respect.

Adapting communication ensures discipline teaches responsibility, not just obedience.

Avoiding Rigid Parenting

Rigid parenting—using the same strategies regardless of age—creates tension. For example, using time-outs with a teenager feels disrespectful and may damage connection. Conversely, giving a toddler too much independence creates overwhelm and chaos.

Flexibility prevents these pitfalls. It shows children that parents respect their growth and trust them with greater responsibility.

A Parent's Inner Challenge

Adapting strategies is often harder for parents than for children. Many parents cling to familiar methods or struggle to let go of control as children grow. Others fear losing authority if they adjust their approach. Reflection helps:

- "Am I adapting to my child's growth, or trying to keep them small?"
- "Do I hold on to control because of fear or habit?"
- "Am I willing to learn and grow alongside my child?"

Parenting requires humility: recognizing that strategies must evolve, and that flexibility is strength, not weakness.

Long-Term Benefits of Adaptation

Children raised with adaptive parenting develop:

- **Confidence:** Trust in their growing independence.
- **Resilience:** Ability to face challenges with evolving skills.
- **Respect:** Appreciation for parents who listen and adjust.
- **Independence:** Readiness for adulthood through gradual responsibility.

By contrast, children raised with rigid or stagnant strategies may rebel, shut down, or struggle with independence.

Final Takeaway

Parenting is a journey of constant adaptation. Children's needs change at every stage, requiring strategies that balance guidance with independence. Parents who adapt—shifting from control to collaboration, from instruction to conversation—raise children who feel respected, empowered, and prepared for adulthood. Adapting strategies is not about losing authority but about guiding wisely as children grow.

Preparing for School and Social Challenges

For many children, school is the first major environment where they encounter expectations, competition, peer dynamics, and performance pressure outside the family. It is also where they begin to navigate friendships, handle conflicts, and develop a sense of identity in a broader community. These experiences bring opportunities for growth but also challenges—academic struggles, peer pressure, bullying, and the complex task of fitting in while staying true to oneself.

Parents play a vital role in preparing children for these challenges. The goal is not to remove obstacles but to equip children with resilience, problem-solving skills, and confidence. A child who knows how to manage setbacks, form healthy relationships, and cope with pressure thrives in school and beyond.

Why Preparation Matters

School is not only about academics. It is a social ecosystem where children learn collaboration, negotiation, and perseverance. Without preparation, children may:

- Feel overwhelmed by academic expectations.
- Struggle with friendships or social rejection.
- Fall prey to peer pressure or bullying.
- Avoid challenges due to fear of failure.

With preparation, children develop:

- **Confidence:** Belief in their ability to cope.
- **Resilience:** Ability to recover from setbacks.
- **Social Intelligence:** Skills to form and sustain relationships.
- **Independence:** Willingness to take responsibility for learning and behavior.

Academic Preparation

Academic challenges often start early—learning to read, mastering math, or completing homework consistently. Parents can support by:

- **Creating Routines:** A consistent study time builds discipline.
- **Breaking Down Tasks:** Teaching children to divide big assignments into smaller steps reduces overwhelm.
- **Encouraging Effort Over Perfection:** Praise persistence, not just grades.
- **Modeling Curiosity:** Show that learning is enjoyable, not just mandatory.

Children thrive when parents emphasize growth, not just results.

Real-World Example: The Struggling Reader

A child finds reading difficult and avoids books.

Scenario A: The parent pressures with criticism: *"You need to try harder!"* The child feels shame and avoids reading more.
Scenario B: The parent reads with the child daily, celebrates progress, and finds fun stories that spark interest. The child gains confidence and persistence.

The second approach prepares the child for academic growth through encouragement, not fear.

Social Preparation

School is also a training ground for social skills. Friendships, teamwork, and conflicts are inevitable. Parents can prepare children by:

- **Modeling Empathy:** Teach children to notice and respect others' feelings.
- **Role-Playing Scenarios:** Practice responses to teasing, invitations, or disagreements.
- **Teaching Assertiveness:** Encourage polite but firm communication: *"I don't like that. Please stop."*
- **Encouraging Inclusion:** Help children see the value of kindness and inclusion in group settings.

Real-World Example: The Playground Disagreement

A child is excluded from a game at recess.

Scenario A: The parent dismisses: *"Don't worry, just play with someone else."* The child feels hurt and unsupported.
Scenario B: The parent validates: *"That sounds painful. What could you say next time to ask to join in?"* The child learns strategies for resilience and social negotiation.

The second response prepares the child to handle future social conflicts with confidence.

Preparing for Peer Pressure

As children grow, peer influence increases. Preparing them involves teaching values and decision-making before challenges arise. Parents can:

- **Discuss Scenarios in Advance:** *"What would you do if a friend pressured you to cheat on a test?"*
- **Encourage Critical Thinking:** Teach children to evaluate consequences.
- **Model Independence:** Show through example that it's okay to go against the crowd.
- **Reinforce Belonging at Home:** A strong family connection reduces the lure of negative peer approval.

Handling Bullying

Bullying is one of the most painful challenges children may face. Preparation involves:

- Teaching children to recognize bullying versus normal conflict.
- Encouraging them to speak up and seek adult help.
- Building confidence so they feel empowered, not powerless.
- Modeling respect and kindness at home to reinforce values.

Parents must listen without judgment and collaborate with schools to ensure safety.

Emotional Preparation

Academic and social challenges often trigger strong emotions—frustration, embarrassment, or anxiety. Parents can help children manage emotions by:

- **Teaching Emotional Vocabulary:** Naming feelings reduces their intensity.
- **Practicing Calming Techniques:** Breathing, visualization, or mindfulness.
- **Normalizing Struggles:** Sharing personal stories of challenges and how they were overcome.
- **Encouraging Persistence:** Reminding children that setbacks are part of growth.

A Parent's Inner Challenge

Parents often struggle with how much to intervene. Some hover, solving every problem, while others step back too much, leaving children unsupported. The balance lies in guiding without rescuing—coaching children through challenges but allowing them to experience natural consequences.

Reflective questions include:

- "Do I solve problems too quickly instead of letting my child try?"
- "Am I preparing my child for resilience, or protecting them from discomfort?"
- "Do I model healthy coping when I face challenges?"

Long-Term Benefits of Preparation

Children prepared for school and social challenges develop:

- **Resilience:** Ability to handle setbacks without collapsing.
- **Confidence:** Belief in their skills to cope with difficulties.
- **Social Competence:** Skills for friendship, teamwork, and conflict resolution.
- **Independence:** Willingness to take ownership of learning and behavior.

By contrast, children unprepared may struggle academically, fear social rejection, or avoid challenges altogether.

Final Takeaway

School and social life present inevitable challenges, but they also offer essential opportunities for growth. Parents cannot remove obstacles, but they can prepare children with the tools to navigate them. Through encouragement, empathy, and practical strategies, parents equip children to handle academics, friendships, and peer pressure with confidence. Preparation does not make challenges disappear—it makes children strong enough to face them.

Teaching Resilience in the Digital Age

The world children grow up in today is vastly different from the one their parents knew. Screens are everywhere—smartphones, tablets, gaming consoles, laptops—and the internet is woven into nearly every aspect of life. Social media shapes friendships, online gaming builds communities, and information flows constantly. While technology brings opportunity, it also presents new challenges: cyberbullying, comparison culture, shortened attention spans, and an overwhelming stream of information.

Parents often worry: *"How will my child cope in such a fast-paced, digital world?"* The answer lies not in shielding children completely from technology but in teaching resilience—the ability to navigate challenges, recover from setbacks, and thrive even in the face of constant change.

Resilience in the digital age is about helping children develop balance, critical thinking, and emotional strength so that technology becomes a tool, not a trap.

Why Resilience Is Essential Today

Children today face unique pressures:

- **Online Comparison:** Social media highlights others' achievements, creating insecurity.
- **Cyberbullying:** Negative comments or exclusion can feel relentless.
- **Instant Gratification:** The constant availability of entertainment makes patience harder.
- **Information Overload:** The internet bombards children with conflicting messages.

- **Digital Dependency:** Excessive screen time can erode real-world skills and relationships.

Without resilience, children may become overwhelmed, anxious, or overly dependent on online validation. With resilience, they learn to balance technology, maintain perspective, and build meaningful offline connections.

The Core Skills of Digital Resilience

To thrive in the digital age, children need:

- **Critical Thinking:** Ability to evaluate online information and distinguish fact from fiction.
- **Emotional Regulation:** Managing feelings triggered by online interactions.
- **Boundaries:** Setting limits around screen time and online activity.
- **Self-Worth:** Confidence rooted in identity, not likes or followers.
- **Adaptability:** Willingness to adjust to rapid changes in technology.

These skills do not emerge automatically; they must be modeled and taught.

Real-World Example: The Social Media Post

A teenager posts a picture online but receives fewer likes than expected.

Scenario A: They feel devastated, delete the post, and vow never to share again.
Scenario B: They reflect, *"Not everyone will react the same way. My value isn't in likes,"* and move forward confidently.

The second outcome demonstrates digital resilience—the ability to face online disappointment without losing self-worth.

Teaching Children to Question Online Content

The internet is filled with misinformation and unrealistic portrayals. Parents can teach critical thinking by asking guiding questions:

- "Who created this content? Why?"
- "Does this source seem reliable?"
- "What might be missing from this picture?"
- "How does this post make you feel, and why?"

Teaching skepticism empowers children to navigate the online world thoughtfully.

Setting Healthy Digital Boundaries

Boundaries protect balance and well-being. Parents can help by:

- Establishing tech-free times, like family meals or before bed.
- Encouraging screen breaks and outdoor play.
- Creating shared rules about device use in common areas.
- Modeling balanced use themselves.

Children who learn boundaries early grow into adults who manage technology, rather than letting technology manage them.

Real-World Example: The Gaming Obsession

A child spends hours on video games, neglecting homework and chores.

Scenario A: The parent bans games entirely, sparking anger and rebellion.
Scenario B: The parent says: *"I know you enjoy gaming. Let's set limits so you can still finish homework and spend time with family."* The child learns balance rather than avoidance.

The second approach teaches responsibility, not resentment.

Building Emotional Resilience Against Online Pressure

Online interactions can be harsh. Children may face exclusion, unkind comments, or pressure to conform. Parents can prepare children by:

- Validating feelings when online interactions hurt.
- Teaching assertive responses to unkind messages.
- Reinforcing self-worth beyond online approval.
- Encouraging offline friendships that provide deeper connection.

Resilience grows when children know they are valued at home regardless of online experiences.

Modeling Digital Balance

Children imitate parents' habits. Parents who constantly check phones send a powerful message about priorities. Modeling digital balance—reading, engaging in hobbies, connecting face-to-face— shows children that life is not lived only on screens.

Avoiding Common Pitfalls

- **Over-Shielding:** Total bans on technology leave children unprepared for real-world digital challenges.
- **Over-Indulgence:** Unlimited access fosters dependency and weakens self-regulation.
- **Hypocrisy:** Enforcing rules children see parents breaking undermines credibility.
- **Ignoring Online Life:** Dismissing digital struggles as "not real" invalidates children's experiences.

A Parent's Inner Challenge

Many parents feel conflicted about technology—they rely on it yet fear its influence. Some avoid addressing it altogether, while others enforce rigid control. Reflection helps parents find balance:

- "Do I model healthy digital habits?"
- "Am I teaching balance, or enforcing control?"
- "Do I acknowledge my child's digital life as real and important?"

Facing these questions helps parents guide with wisdom instead of fear.

Long-Term Benefits of Digital Resilience

Children who build resilience in the digital age develop:

- **Confidence:** Ability to handle online pressure without losing self-worth.
- **Balance:** Healthy habits around screen time and offline activities.
- **Critical Thinking:** Skills to question content and resist manipulation.
- **Emotional Strength:** Tools to cope with online rejection or negativity.
- **Independence:** Readiness to navigate digital spaces responsibly.

By contrast, children without resilience may become anxious, overly dependent on online approval, or vulnerable to harmful influences.

Final Takeaway

The digital age is not going away. Children must learn not just how to use technology but how to thrive within it. Teaching digital resilience means preparing children to think critically, set boundaries, and regulate emotions in an online world. Parents who embrace this challenge raise children who see technology as a tool, not a measure of self-worth. In the end, digital resilience equips children not only to survive but to thrive in a world that is constantly connected.

Maintaining Strong Parent–Child Bonds in Teen Years

The teenage years often come with warnings: "Brace yourself," "Good luck surviving," or "They won't want to talk to you anymore." Parents hear stories of slammed doors, rolled eyes, and children who once clung to them now demanding independence. While adolescence does bring new challenges, it does not have to mean broken bonds. In fact, maintaining strong parent–child connections during the teen years is not only possible but essential.

Teenagers crave independence, but they also need security. They may push away on the surface, yet underneath they still long for guidance, acceptance, and love. Parents who adapt their relationship strategies during these years provide the foundation for trust that carries into adulthood.

Why Bonds Matter More Than Ever in Adolescence

Adolescence is a season of identity formation, emotional intensity, and social experimentation. Teens face pressures from peers, academics, and the digital world. They wrestle with self-doubt, shifting moods, and big questions about who they are and who they want to be.

Strong parental bonds provide:

- **Security:** A safe base to return to amid external pressures.
- **Guidance:** Trusted voices to balance peer influence.
- **Confidence:** Affirmation of worth and identity.

- **Resilience:** Emotional support that helps teens handle setbacks.

Without strong bonds, teens may seek belonging in riskier places or feel isolated in their struggles.

The Shift From Control to Connection

During early childhood, parents provide structure through rules and guidance. As children grow, the relationship must shift. By adolescence, excessive control often leads to rebellion or secrecy. The focus should move from control to connection—building trust, respect, and open communication.

Instead of dictating every choice, parents become mentors, coaches, and allies. This shift allows teens to practice independence while still knowing they are supported.

Real-World Example: The Late-Night Party

A teenager asks to attend a late-night party.

Scenario A: The parent says, *"Absolutely not. Don't even think about it."* The teen feels controlled and may lie to attend anyway. Scenario B: The parent says, *"Let's talk about it. What's the plan for safety? Who's going? How will you get home?"* The teen feels respected, and a compromise is reached.

The second approach preserves trust and keeps communication open.

How to Maintain Bonds With Teens

1. **Listen More Than You Lecture:** Teens often need space to vent without immediate solutions. Listening shows respect and builds trust.
2. **Respect Their Privacy:** Knock before entering rooms, keep confidences, and avoid over-snooping unless safety is at risk.

3. **Share Your Own Struggles:** Teens respect authenticity. Sharing stories of your mistakes and lessons learned builds relatability.
4. **Create Rituals of Connection:** Family dinners, shared hobbies, or car rides without distractions become safe spaces for conversation.
5. **Validate Feelings:** Instead of dismissing moods as "dramatic," acknowledge them. *"I can see you're really stressed about this test."*
6. **Encourage Independence:** Allow increasing responsibility, while remaining available for support.

Balancing Boundaries and Freedom

Strong bonds do not mean abandoning boundaries. Teens still need limits to feel secure. The key is setting boundaries collaboratively. For example:

- Curfews can be negotiated rather than imposed.
- Screen time rules can be discussed based on mutual respect.
- Household responsibilities can be shared rather than dictated.

Collaborative boundaries teach responsibility and reinforce respect in the relationship.

Real-World Example: The Missed Curfew

A teen comes home late.

Scenario A: The parent explodes: *"You're grounded for a month!"* The teen feels punished, not understood.
Scenario B: The parent calmly says: *"You missed curfew. I was worried. Let's talk about how to rebuild trust."* The teen feels accountable but respected.

The second response strengthens bonds instead of eroding them.

Supporting Teens Through Identity Formation

Adolescence is a time of experimentation with identity—clothes, music, hobbies, beliefs. Parents who criticize or mock these explorations risk damaging trust. Instead, they can express curiosity: *"Tell me what you like about this style or music."* Respecting identity exploration communicates unconditional acceptance.

Technology and Connection

Digital life often competes with parent–teen relationships. Yet technology can also be a bridge. Parents can:

- Show interest in their teen's online world without judgment.
- Share media experiences—watching shows, playing games, or listening to music together.
- Use technology as a conversation starter rather than a battleground.

Staying engaged in the digital world shows that parents respect what matters to their teen.

Avoiding Common Pitfalls

- **Overreacting:** Dramatic responses to mistakes push teens toward secrecy.
- **Overcontrolling:** Excessive rules stifle independence and damage trust.
- **Disengaging:** Withdrawing when teens pull away creates emotional distance.
- **Invalidating:** Dismissing feelings as trivial undermines confidence.

A Parent's Inner Challenge

Parents often grieve the shift from childhood closeness to teenage independence. They may feel rejected or unneeded. Yet distance is not rejection—it is growth. Reflective questions include:

- "Am I clinging to control instead of building connection?"
- "Do I take my teen's independence personally?"
- "Am I creating safe spaces for my teen to come to me?"

Accepting the evolving relationship helps parents stay close even as teens seek freedom.

Long-Term Benefits of Strong Bonds

Teens who maintain strong bonds with parents grow into adults who:

- Trust themselves and others.
- Make healthier decisions, less influenced by negative peer pressure.
- Return to parents for guidance even in adulthood.
- Build strong, respectful relationships with partners and peers.
- Carry resilience from knowing they are unconditionally loved.

Teens without strong bonds may become isolated, rebellious, or overly dependent on peers for validation.

Final Takeaway

The teenage years do not have to break parent–child bonds. In fact, they can strengthen them if parents adapt—shifting from control to connection, from lecturing to listening, from enforcing to guiding. By respecting independence while maintaining love and boundaries, parents remain trusted allies. Strong bonds in adolescence lay the foundation for lifelong connection, ensuring that even as children grow into adults, they never outgrow the security of their parents' love.

Raising Strong Kids Into Strong Adults

Parenting does not end when children turn eighteen. While the intensity of daily care may lessen, the ultimate goal of parenting is lifelong: raising children who grow into adults capable of resilience, responsibility, empathy, and confidence. Every stage of childhood is preparation for adulthood, where the lessons learned at home are tested in the wider world.

Raising strong adults means more than preparing children for careers or academic success. It means shaping character, values, and life skills that endure across circumstances. Strength is not measured by dominance or control, but by the ability to navigate challenges, build relationships, and contribute positively to society.

Defining Strength in Adulthood

Parents sometimes imagine strength as toughness—never crying, never struggling, never needing help. True strength is far deeper. A strong adult is:

- **Resilient:** Able to recover from setbacks.
- **Responsible:** Accountable for choices and their consequences.
- **Independent:** Capable of managing life without overdependence.
- **Empathetic:** Aware of others' needs and compassionate in response.
- **Authentic:** Grounded in values rather than swayed by external pressures.

These qualities grow gradually, through consistent parenting choices and everyday experiences.

The Parent's Long-Term Role

Parents are not raising children for childhood—they are raising them for adulthood. This requires long-term vision. Decisions about discipline, boundaries, communication, and values are not just about today's behavior but about the person the child is becoming.

For example:

- Teaching accountability for chores builds responsibility for future work.
- Encouraging decision-making develops independence in college or careers.
- Modeling empathy fosters compassionate friendships and partnerships.
- Allowing failure builds resilience for adult setbacks.

Every small moment of parenting contributes to the larger goal of shaping a strong adult.

Real-World Example: The First Job

A teenager struggles with their first part-time job, forgetting shifts and making mistakes.

Scenario A: The parent rescues—calling the manager, excusing the teen, or minimizing the responsibility. The teen avoids accountability and remains unprepared for adulthood.
Scenario B: The parent says: *"This is part of learning. What steps can you take to be more reliable?"* The teen reflects, adjusts, and gains confidence through growth.

The second scenario builds strength through accountability and ownership.

Preparing for Independence

Strong adults must navigate independence—managing money, balancing time, caring for themselves. Parents can prepare children by gradually teaching life skills:

- **Financial Literacy:** Saving, budgeting, and distinguishing wants from needs.
- **Time Management:** Balancing responsibilities and leisure.
- **Problem-Solving:** Tackling obstacles without panic.
- **Self-Care:** Maintaining health, rest, and emotional well-being.

These skills cannot be learned overnight at eighteen. They grow through responsibility given over time.

Balancing Support and Autonomy

Parents often struggle with the transition to adulthood. Some cling too tightly, rescuing even into adulthood. Others withdraw too soon, leaving children unsupported. The balance is providing guidance without control—remaining a safe base while allowing independence.

For example, a parent may help a college student brainstorm solutions to stress but resist solving everything for them. This balance communicates: *"I trust you to handle life, but I'm here if you need me."*

Real-World Example: The Apartment Search

A young adult moves out for the first time and struggles to find affordable housing.

Scenario A: The parent takes over completely, handling all details. The child gains housing but not independence.
Scenario B: The parent offers guidance—helping brainstorm, reviewing budgets, asking reflective questions—but leaves the final decision to the child. The child learns resilience and ownership.

The second scenario prepares the child for adulthood with both skill and confidence.

Avoiding Common Pitfalls

- **Overprotection:** Shielding children from struggle leaves them unprepared for adult realities.
- **Overcontrol:** Micromanaging decisions prevents independence.
- **Neglect:** Withdrawing too soon leaves children unsupported.
- **Equating Success With Wealth or Status:** Narrow definitions of strength overlook character, resilience, and relationships.

The Importance of Lifelong Values

Skills matter, but values anchor strong adulthood. Parents who model and teach honesty, empathy, responsibility, and perseverance give their children internal compasses. In adulthood, when external rules fade, these values guide decisions.

Conversations about values—respect, kindness, integrity—should be ongoing. More important, parents must live these values daily. Children learn more from what parents model than from what they preach.

Real-World Example: Integrity at Work

A child sees their parent admit a mistake at work rather than hiding it. The child learns that strength includes honesty and accountability. Years later, as an adult, they carry the same integrity into their career.

Values passed through example endure longer than any lecture.

Preparing for Lifelong Relationships

Strong adults do not just succeed individually—they build meaningful relationships. Parents can prepare children by modeling healthy communication, conflict resolution, and respect in the home. Teaching children to listen, empathize, and repair relationships after conflict equips them for friendships, partnerships, and parenting in their own future.

A Parent's Inner Challenge

Parents often face their own fears when raising children for adulthood:

- Fear of letting go.
- Fear of their child failing.
- Fear of losing closeness.

Yet letting go is not losing connection. A child who grows into a strong adult often returns with deeper respect and gratitude. Reflection helps:

- "Am I preparing my child for independence, or clinging out of fear?"
- "Do I define strength by external success or by character?"
- "Am I willing to grow and adapt as my child becomes an adult?"

Strong adults emerge when parents embrace their evolving role—not as controllers but as guides, mentors, and supporters.

Long-Term Benefits

Children raised to become strong adults grow into individuals who:

- Take responsibility for their lives.
- Build resilient relationships.
- Contribute positively to communities.
- Adapt to challenges with confidence.
- Live authentically, rooted in values.

By contrast, children who are overprotected, overcontrolled, or unsupported may enter adulthood unprepared, insecure, or disconnected.

Final Takeaway

Raising strong kids into strong adults is the ultimate goal of parenting. It is not about producing perfection but about preparing for resilience, independence, empathy, and authenticity. Every choice parents make—from discipline to encouragement, from boundaries to freedom—contributes to this long-term vision.

Strength in adulthood is not measured by wealth or power but by the ability to face life with courage, integrity, and compassion. Parents who nurture these qualities give their children the greatest gift: not just a strong childhood but a strong future.

A Note of Thanks

Thank you for taking the time to read this book. My hope is that it has offered you insight, encouragement, and practical tools to support your journey as a parent. Every small step you take toward connection, resilience, and growth makes a lasting difference in your child's life.

If you found value in these pages, I would be deeply grateful if you left a positive review. Your feedback not only supports this work but also helps other parents discover it, giving them the chance to find encouragement and guidance when they need it most.

Together, we can build a world where every child has the chance to grow with strength, confidence, and love.

-Eric LeBouthillier

www.ingramcontent.com/pod-product-compliance
Lightning Source LLC
Chambersburg PA
CBHW061730120626
46550CB00005B/1761